Hiking
Ruins Seldom Seen

Dave Wilson

FALCON®

Guilford, Connecticut
An imprint of The Globe Pequot Press

A FALCON GUIDE ®

Copyright © 1999 by The Globe Pequot Press
Previously published by Falcon Publishing, Inc.

Project Editor: David Lee
Production Editor: Jessica Solberg
Copyeditor: Heath Silberfeld
Maps by: Chris Salcedo
Page Compositor: Dana Kim-Wincapaw
Book design by Falcon Publishing, Inc.

Library of Congress Cataloging-in-Publication Data

Wilson, Dave, 1965–
  Hiking ruins seldom seen / Dave Wilson
      p. cm.
  Includes bibliographical references (p.   ) and index.
  ISBN 1-56044-834-2 (pbk.)
  1. Indians of North America—Southwest, New—Antiquities—Guidebooks. 2. Hiking—Southwest, New—Guidebooks. 3. Southwest, New—Antiquities—Guidebooks. I. Title.

E78.S7W58 1999
917.904'33—dc21

99-35783
CIP

CAUTION
Outdoor recreational activities are by their very nature potentially hazardous. All participants in such activities must assume the responsibility for their own actions and safety. The information contained in this guidebook cannot replace sound judgment and good decision-making skills, which help reduce risk exposure, nor does the scope of this book allow for disclosure of all the potential hazards and risks involved in such activities.

Learn as much as possible about the outdoor recreational activities in which you participate, prepare for the unexpected, and be cautious. The reward will be a safer and more enjoyable experience.

Contents

For Thelma. Thanks for exploring every nook and cranny of Arizona, traveling to several other states, heading deep into Mexico, venturing across the ocean, and just hanging out with me for 10 years. You were an excellent person with whom to see the world, and you will be my friend forever.

Acknowledgments

Special thanks to J. Scott Wood, Forest Archaeologist for Tonto National Forest, for his invaluable critique of the Arizona section of this book and for his support of this publication. Thanks also to archaeologists with Grand Canyon National Park, Gila National Forest, Santa Fe National Forest, Manti-La Sal National Forest, Canyonlands National Park, and several Bureau of Land Management offices in southern Utah for their input and/or reviews of chapters of the book pertaining to their respective districts.

Overview Map

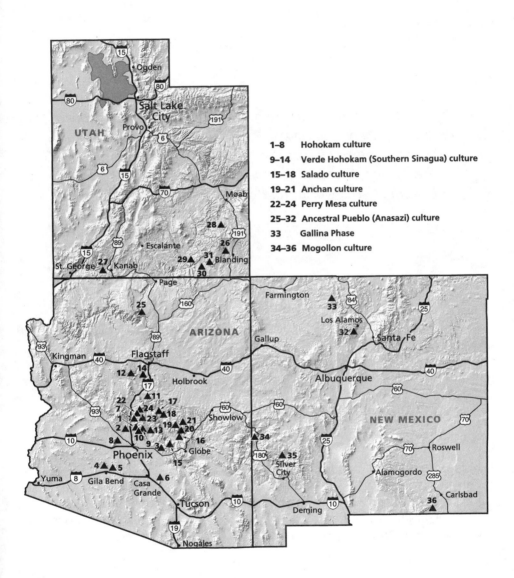

1–8   Hohokam culture

9–14   Verde Hohokam (Southern Sinagua) culture

15–18   Salado culture

19–21   Anchan culture

22–24   Perry Mesa culture

25–32   Ancestral Pueblo (Anasazi) culture

33   Gallina Phase

34–36   Mogollon culture

Map Legend

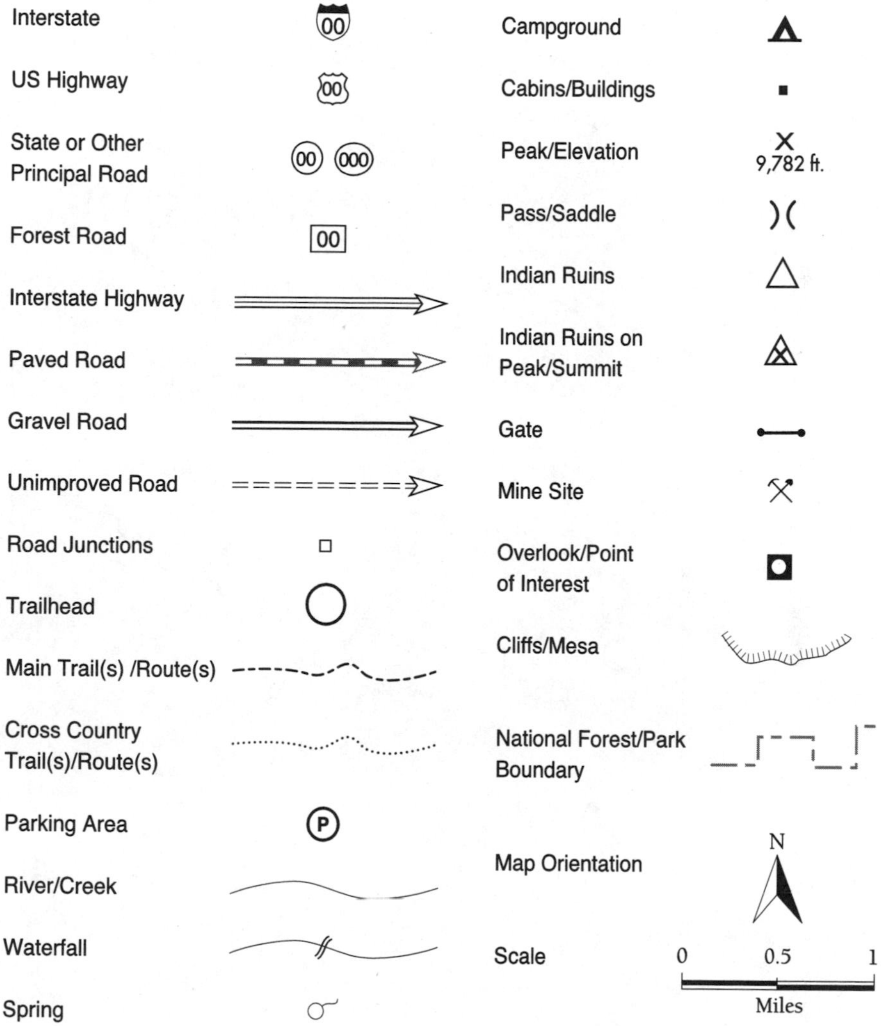

Interstate	(00)	Campground	▲
US Highway	(00)	Cabins/Buildings	▪
State or Other Principal Road	(00) (000)	Peak/Elevation	✕ 9,782 ft.
Forest Road	[00]	Pass/Saddle	)(
Interstate Highway	⟹	Indian Ruins	△
Paved Road	⟹	Indian Ruins on Peak/Summit	⧊
Gravel Road	⟹	Gate	•—•
Unimproved Road	=====⟹	Mine Site	⚒
Road Junctions	▫	Overlook/Point of Interest	◼
Trailhead	◯	Cliffs/Mesa	⌣⟨⟨⟨⟨⟩
Main Trail(s) /Route(s)	– – – – –	National Forest/Park Boundary	⌐ ⌐
Cross Country Trail(s)/Route(s)	··········		
Parking Area	(P)	Map Orientation	N ↑
River/Creek	～～		
Waterfall	～//～	Scale	0 0.5 1 Miles
Spring	�		

Introduction

On a Saturday afternoon in 1993, my wife and I stood sweating in a remote patch of desert near the city of Casa Grande, Arizona. We had driven all the way from my home in Phoenix to see what a certain "off-the-beaten-path" outdoor guidebook had described as an "Indian pueblo" with a nearby "artifact scatter." We could find neither. The book's hand-drawn map of the area was as lacking in detail as the written description of the place. At one point I thought I found a piece of pottery but eventually realized it was a fragment of clay pigeon blasted apart by a shotgun. We decided to go home.

A couple of days later I went to the bookstore to find a better "off-the-beaten-path" field guide. I wanted something that focused entirely on lesser known, remotely located Native American ruins and rock art sites. I wanted something written for the general public, not archaeologists or anthropologists. I wanted the book to have detailed maps, good descriptions and photos, and enough interpretive information so readers could understand basic points—which Native Americans made the ruins, when they built them, and what purpose the ancient buildings served. However, I could find no such publication. I checked several other bookstores and the library, but there was no good field guide about Native American ruins.

My initial interest in Native American ruins was simply an extension of my love for the outdoors. I hike. I fish. I photograph wildlife. I think most people who spend a lot of time in the outdoors develop a fascination with Native Americans of the past. After all, the Native Americans *lived* in the outdoors. It seemed to me that if these people left ancient ruins out in the desert, the prehistoric buildings would make interesting hiking destinations.

I am also a writer. Mainly I write promotional copy for public relations-type agencies and corporations. However, after wandering around the desert on that hot day in 1993, and after realizing there were no good books about remotely located Native American ruins, I decided I should combine my interests in writing and the outdoors and create the publication I could not find at the bookstore. I should be the first person in Arizona to write a good book about Native American ruins and rock art sites located off the beaten path.

I have nothing against popular, easily accessible, prehistoric Native American ruins that have been developed for public interpretation. The ancient buildings at such places and the exhibits near them are always interesting and provide great opportunities to learn about early Native Americans. However, I don't enjoy visiting protected sites nearly as much as I like heading into the wilderness and exploring places that are not surrounded by fences or sidewalks. I could explain why and talk about things like "adventure" and an enhanced sense of "discovery," but if I have to explain why I prefer the wilder places then you will never truly understand. I just do, and I believe there are a significant number of people out there who share the same attitude. With that in mind, I decided that every archaeological site in my book should meet the following criteria:

1. The site should be located remotely enough to make it a good hiking destination.

2. The site should not have any sort of modern development around it, nor should there be any interpretive guides or signs present.

I also added the following two criteria for reasons that should be obvious:

3. The ruin or rock art site should be large and well-preserved enough to be interesting and worth the trip.

4. The site should be on public land.

After working on the project for a while, I felt the need to narrow the historical scope of the book to a certain time period and eventually added one more criterion:

5. The site should belong to one of the agriculturally based "high cultures" that lived in the American Southwest between roughly the year zero and A.D. 1400.

After I got into the project, I found it very difficult to find a large number of archaeological sites that satisfied every single criterion. I stuck to the original plan as best I could, but I ended up including a few sites that don't require a lot of hiking, and even one that requires none at all. However, all the ruins and rock art sites described in this book are worth seeing, all are basically off the beaten path, and the majority of them actually do meet all five of my criteria.

When I started the book, I knew almost nothing about ruins or the Native Americans who left them behind. I figured I would learn as I went, and I did. I spent as much time sifting through research papers at university libraries as I did hiking in the desert, and I spoke with quite a few archaeologists. Although I have learned a lot, I still do not claim to be an expert on Native American history. I approached this project as a writer and a hiker, not as a scientist, and that is still who I am.

This drawing depicts a lizard petroglyph, one of the more prominent images at the rock art site in the Gila Bend Mountains.

In 1993, my plan had been to write only about Native American ruins within 100 miles of Phoenix. I figured the whole project would take about a year. Five years later I was wandering all over Utah and New Mexico looking for prehistoric buildings. In doing so, I explored places I never would have gone if I was hiking just for the fun of hiking. Armed with a Global Positioning System (GPS) receiver and an assortment of topo maps, I ventured into obscure patches of Bureau of Land Management (BLM) land where there are no trails and one can wander for days without encountering another person. I saw places like Canyonlands National Park, which, although not obscure, probably never would have crossed my mind as a destination if I wasn't on a quest for cliff dwellings. The archaeological sites I found were spectacular, but I discovered much more than Native American ruins. I found places in southern Utah that looked like heaven on earth—where reddish canyons snaked their way though vast expanses of sagebrush while snowcapped mountains loomed in the distance. From the highways of New Mexico, I saw mountains, small towns, and old buildings that seemed to jump right out of Georgia O'Keeffe paintings. I saw a bear, walked right up to a coyote puppy, and watched a partial eclipse of the moon from a chilly, windswept summit.

In the process of researching the book, by 1998 I had also been detained and searched by U.S. Border Patrol agents; nearly run off the highway by a trucker twice, reported it to police, and ended up in handcuffs when the trucker's buddies flipped the story around; and, in what seemed like a scene out of the classic Western *Shane,* encountered a couple of belligerent, whiskey-drinking cowboys at a bar in Glenwood, New Mexico, where I ordered a Sprite. I almost stepped on a rattlesnake and nearly got trampled to death by an angry cow. I discovered just how destitute most modern-day Native Americans really are.

Looking back on it, I didn't just write a book: I went on an odyssey. I'm glad to be home now, unharmed, with no criminal record and with no regrets. Even though my travels are complete, though, one very important question remains: Was it really a good idea to write a book like this in the first place, or will it do more harm than good?

Since the beginning, I have been aware that my book would be available not only to responsible, law-abiding individuals but to vandals and pothunters who might set out to destroy the archaeological sites. However, people whose primary interest is theft or vandalism do not have a great appreciation of ruins. Those who do not have a great appreciation of ruins will not spend their hard-earned money to buy this book, nor will they put forth the time and effort required to reach most of the sites that I have described. In fact, most thieves and vandals don't even head into the wilderness with the purpose of finding ruins. They stumble upon them accidentally, and they have no idea what they have discovered. I sincerely believe that only people with a legitimate interest in archaeology and a good appreciation of Native American ruins will be sufficiently motivated to invest the time, effort, and money required to buy this book and visit the sites described within.

This book can be enjoyed by both amateur archaeologists and those who enjoy heading into the wilderness. I hope you enjoy it, and I trust you will give these ruins the respect they deserve.

NATIVE AMERICAN RUINS AND THE LAW

A variety of state and federal laws protect the archaeological resources described in this book. These include, but are not limited to, the Archaeological Resources Protection Act (ARPA) and the Arizona Antiquities Act.

ARPA prohibits the removal of pottery and all other artifacts from archaeological sites on federal land, including national forests, national parks, and BLM land. ARPA also prohibits the destruction of ruins themselves and the defacing or removal of rock art.

Pothunters and vandals can be fined up to $10,000 or imprisoned for up to one year, or both. If the value of the archaeological resources involved and the cost of their restoration and repair exceed $500, the perpetrator may be charged with a felony, the fine increased to up to $20,000, and the prison time increased to up to two years. Repeat offenders may be fined up to $100,000 or imprisoned for up to five years, or both.

Note that under this law a person only has to steal or damage $500 worth of archaeological resources to be charged with a felony. That means it wouldn't take a heck of a lot of theft or vandalism to drain your bank account, put you away for a long time, and ruin all job applications for the rest of your life.

In addition to fines and prison time, the cost of restoring and repairing damaged archaeological resources can be billed to the perpetrator. The government can also seize all tools and vehicles used by a vandal or pothunter during the commission of the offense.

ARPA allows qualified people, such as archaeologists, to obtain permits from a federal land manager to excavate ruins and remove artifacts for scientific research. ARPA also allows Native American tribes to make their own laws about archaeological resources located on reservations. However, if a tribe does not make its own laws, ARPA applies to that tribe's land.

Just for the record, I want to tell you this: The first person ever convicted as a criminal under ARPA was a man who got caught stealing Hohokam artifacts from an archaeological site on the Tonto National Forest.

Arrowheads on the surface of the ground (as opposed to buried) are not protected under ARPA. This has led to a common misconception that it is legal to collect them. While arrowheads on the surface may be exempt from this piece of legislation, they are still protected under lesser-known federal laws and regulations, and if you take one home you can be charged with a misdemeanor and fined up to $500.

The Arizona Antiquities Act prohibits collecting pottery and other artifacts on state land without a permit. Violators who remove sherds from the surface of the ground can be fined up to $1,000 and sentenced to up to six months in jail. Violators who excavate an archaeological site (dig beneath the surface) can be charged with a felony, fined up to $150,000, and sentenced to up to two years in prison. Repeat offenders can be fined up to $150,000 and sentenced to up to seven years in prison.

The Arizona act also prohibits damaging or defacing petroglyphs. Those who do so can be fined up to $750 and sentenced to up to four months in jail.

Utah and New Mexico also have state laws protecting archaeological resources. However, none of the Utah and New Mexico sites described in this book are on state land.

ETIQUETTE AT ARCHAEOLOGICAL SITES

The first rule at any archaeological site should be to enjoy it. Native American ruins are fascinating places to explore and provide visitors with a unique combination of mystery and intellectual stimulation. Many are also surrounded by wildlife and beautiful scenery and make great hiking destinations.

However, archaeological sites are also a very fragile part of the Southwest's heritage and can easily be damaged. Please practice proper etiquette while visiting prehistoric pueblos, cliff dwellings, and rock art sites.

Do Not Lean, Climb, or Walk on Walls or Roofs

Prehistoric walls and roofs are very fragile and can easily collapse under your weight. Be especially careful where you step when exploring poorly preserved pueblos. It is very easy to walk on top of low, crumbling stone walls without even realizing it.

Do Not Pick Up an Artifact, Then Place It Somewhere Else

At many ruins you will find piles of pottery or stone tools that previous hikers have collected and placed together in one spot for display. While most people who do this mean no harm, they do not understand that archaeologists can obtain valuable information not only from what they find but from where they find it.

Do Not Touch Rock Art

Even the slightest amount of oil from a human hand or finger can erode petroglyphs and cause the delicate pigments in pictographs to disintegrate.

Do Not Chalk Rock Art

Some people outline petroglyphs and pictographs with chalk so they will show up better in a photograph. This is usually done with the belief that the chalk will soon weather away and leave the rock art unharmed. Research over the decades has shown that chalk often lasts far longer than anticipated and can even cause permanent damage.

Do Not Build a Fire Inside an Alcove

If there is rock art inside an alcove, smoke from a fire can blacken it almost immediately. Fires can also damage ancient buildings. Even if there is no

5

evidence of prehistoric occupation in an alcove, remains may exist below the surface.

Do Not Take Pottery

The temptation to pocket a piece of pottery can be great, but there are many negative consequences of doing so. Please see the following section to learn about the many reasons why pottery should be left where you find it.

REASONS NOT TO TAKE POTTERY

You will not find any intact bowls or pots at any of the ruins in this book. However, you may find small potsherds at many of the sites. Please consider the following points if you're ever tempted to take one home.

Taking Pottery Is Illegal

State and federal laws prohibit the removal of pottery or any other artifacts from Native American ruins. Violators can be given stiff fines, or be sentenced to jail or prison, or both. See the Native American Ruins and the Law earlier in this chapter to learn more about laws protecting archaeological resources and the penalties provided for pothunters and vandals.

Stealing Pottery Robs Archaeologists of Important Information

Different cultures used different types of pottery during different periods of prehistory. Archaeologists can therefore use the ceramics they find at a ruin to determine the site's cultural affiliation and date of occupation. Other information obtained from pottery includes insights into trade relationships, since pots and bowls were often among the objects traded.

All of the ruins in this book have been recorded or surveyed, but not all of them have been excavated or even studied in depth on the surface. As a result, relatively little is known about many of them, and archaeologists may return one day to find out more. If they do, they'll want to see whatever pottery is left.

Stealing Pottery Robs Other Hikers of the Opportunity to See It

If you take home pottery, you won't just be stealing information from archaeologists. You'll also be robbing other people just like yourself of the opportunity to see it. Leave every piece where you find it so the next hiker can experience the ruin exactly the same way you did.

Most People Are Not Impressed with Potsherds

The fact that you're reading the words on this page indicates you have a certain fascination with prehistoric pottery. Consider, however, that most people in the world do not. If they did, the general public would spend more money on maps and hiking boots than beer and heavy-metal CDs. Most people to whom you plan to show off your pottery will not be nearly as impressed as you might expect. Sure, they'll ask if the stuff is real and muster up just enough interest to make you happy, but the great majority of people just won't care. Save yourself the disappointment and leave the sherds for other hikers who really do think pottery is worth seeing.

If you do have a friend who might think pottery is interesting, ask him or her if they would like to accompany you on your next hiking trip and discover some sherds for themselves. If they don't want to come along, they fail the enthusiasm test and won't really care if you bring back sherds for them to see.

There Is an Alternative to Stealing Pottery

If you want a souvenir of your visit to a Native American ruin, don't steal pottery: Take photographs. Good pictures have a surprisingly satisfying effect on your friends, coworkers, and, most importantly, yourself. In fact, photos make a much greater impression on people than potsherds do because photos reveal much more about a ruin than small pieces of pottery can. Only pictures can illustrate prehistoric walls two stories high and ancient doorways so tiny that nobody would believe your descriptions without proof. You can also capture petroglyphs on film and, if you like, small artifacts such as broken metates, mortar holes, and even pieces of pottery.

Many people also like to draw potsherds, especially decorated ones. This is a relatively easy thing to do, even for people who are not artists.

If you decide to take pictures you may want to read the following section for some tips on photographing archaeological sites.

PHOTOGRAPHY TIPS

Photography is a great way to record your trips to Native American ruins. In fact, a good shot of a pueblo, cliff dwelling, or petroglyph makes a far better souvenir than a stolen potsherd. The following tips may help you take better pictures.

Tips for Photographing Ruins

Use a Wide-angle Lens for Most Shots
The steep terrain surrounding many ruins makes it difficult to back away from them far enough to frame everything you want in a picture. For example, if you try to step back 50 feet from a cliff dwelling to get an entire building into the photo, you might step right off the edge of a cliff. Since you'll be forced to take most of your pictures up close, you'll need a wide-angle lens for most shots. A 28 mm or 35 mm lens usually works best. A 50 mm lens will do if that's all you have, but in most cases you don't want to go any higher than that. Most "point-and-shoot" cameras with fixed lenses have wide-angle optics built into them.

There are, of course, exceptions to this rule, and some ruins have vantage points nearby from which you can snap a good shot with a telephoto lens. Individual ruin descriptions in this book contain photo tips that will tell you when a telephoto lens is needed.

Put Something in the Photo for Size Reference
People often have difficulty getting an accurate perception of size when they look at photographs of a ruin. Exceptionally tall walls may not look so impressive, and tiny doorways can appear to be normal height. To remedy this problem, put something in the photo for size reference. Hats and backpacks work nicely. People work even better because they add a little life to the picture, and you can have them point or look at something in the photo that might otherwise not get noticed.

The same holds true for pottery, metates, and mortar holes. Lay a compass, pair of sunglasses, or set of keys next to a small artifact and people will easily be able to tell how big it is. Rock art seems to be the exception to the rule. Unless a petroglyph is exceptionally large or small, it will probably photograph well without a foreign object for size reference.

Take Many Pictures
Crumbling old ruins can be extremely tricky subjects to photograph. Hilltop sites, which often lack tall walls, will place an especially high demand on your photography skills. Shots you think will turn out great often end up looking like piles of rocks, and shots you didn't expect to be so impressive sometimes turn out great. The only real way to ensure you get a good shot of a ruin is to take a whole bunch of them. Shoot every major feature at a ruin, and take each shot from a variety of angles. Don't be afraid to use up an entire roll of film at a single site. After the roll is developed, you'll appreciate the opportunity to sift through all the pictures and keep only the ones you like.

Pack Camera Equipment Properly
You can't take good pictures with a broken camera, so take adequate precautions to protect all your photography equipment. Cameras and lenses get banged around an awful lot while hiking to ruins, so pack them in something shockproof. If you don't want to pay for a shockproof camera case, make one yourself. A coffee can or large covered plastic bowl padded on the inside with rags works great. Rain can also ruin your equipment, so pack a large plastic bag into which you can put your camera in case bad weather strikes. Of course, if you use the plastic bowl trick, you won't need the bag.

Tips for Photographing Petroglyphs

When photographing a petroglyph, the primary objective is to create as much contrast between the drawing and the surrounding rock as possible. In other words, the ancient image must show up in the picture. Following are some tips for maximizing contrast.

Photograph in Soft Light
Intense midday sunlight has a way of flushing out petroglyphs, causing them to blend in with the surrounding rock. You'll get much better results if you take pictures in the soft light of early morning or late afternoon. Petroglyphs also photograph well in the shade and on dry overcast days.

If you find a petroglyph bathed in harsh light but don't want to wait around until conditions change, then have a friend create a "hood" over the subject by holding a shirt, jacket, or some other wide object over it. If you frame the glyph tightly, the photo will not show whatever is used to cast the shadow. Just be careful not to touch the artwork while doing this.

Photograph from the Best Angle
The best angle from which to shoot a petroglyph is not always straight on. Take a few steps to the left of the image, then a few steps to the right. In many cases the contrast will change as you move from one side of the image to the other. The change is often very subtle, but it can sometimes be dramatic enough to make or break a photo. This phenomenon has something to do with the way the sunlight plays off the natural relief of the rock, but it is not really necessary to understand why it happens. Simply take your picture from the angle that provides the most striking image. The best angle for any given petroglyph changes constantly with the season and time of day.

Photograph in Dry Weather
Always shoot petroglyphs when the weather is dry because water on the rocks can make prehistoric drawings disappear almost completely. Even a soft sprinkle can cause rock art to fade into its surroundings. Also keep in mind that on cool overcast days, the rocks may remain wet for hours after a good rain.

This is a drawing of a petroglyph near the Gila Bend ruin. An obvious interpretation of the rock art would be that it depicts a flower. However, it also bears a striking resemblance to another petroglyph about 30 miles down the Gila River that has been interpreted by one archaeologist as the sun.

Water can make rock art so difficult to see that you may not want to visit petroglyph sites on rainy days even if you do not plan to take any pictures. As mentioned, however, *dry* overcast days make for good photos.

Tips for Photographing Pictographs

Most pictographs that have survived over the centuries are located in caves or alcoves where they are protected from rain and direct sunlight. The soft, even light in such places usually makes photographing them relatively easy. The only exception is when a cave or alcove is so deep that there isn't much light at all, in which case a flash, high-speed film, or time exposure may be required. It is rare, however, to find a pictograph that cannot be adequately photographed in the middle of the day with ASA 400 film.

All of the above are general tips. Since conditions vary from place to place, many of the descriptions in this book include photo tips that apply specifically to the site described. If no photo tip is provided, I encountered no challenging or unusual conditions when I visited the site.

HAZARDS

Seeking remote prehistoric places can be a lot of fun, but hiking to Native American ruins includes a certain amount of danger just like backpacking, mountain biking, canoeing, and other outdoor activities. If you use common sense and plan your trips well, you should not encounter any problems, but be aware that some hazards, such as the following, do exist.

This drawing depicts one of the more animated rock art scenes near the Gila Bend ruin. Images like this defy interpretation.

Dehydration and Heat Exhaustion

Perhaps the greatest risks to your health when hiking to Native American ruins are dehydration and heat exhaustion, especially during the summer. Many of the hikes in this book are quite difficult. Pace yourself accordingly and carry plenty of water. Remember, you can always dump excess water if you find you don't need it, but you cannot always obtain more if you begin to overheat or suffer from dehydration.

Dirt Roads

Driving on dirt roads can also be hazardous. Tires can get stuck in mud, soft sand, and deep ruts, and big rocks can smash oil pans, transmissions, and other vehicle parts. The best way to avoid problems is simply to call it quits when you no longer feel comfortable with a steadily deteriorating road. Remember, just because a road gets bad doesn't mean you have to end the journey. It just means you have to park and start walking.

Also note that road conditions change constantly. A good rainfall can turn what is normally a smooth and well-maintained dirt road into a muddy mess. Rain can also cause the water level in creeks and washes crossing over roads to rise to dangerously high levels. Other factors such as lack of use or maintenance also cause road conditions to change over time. This book gives a general idea of what road conditions were like on *dry* days between 1993 and 1998, but due to inevitable changes at the hands of both

Rattlesnakes, like this one at the base of Skull Mesa in Arizona, are a fairly common sight in and around Native American ruins.

humans and nature, you must be the ultimate judge of whether or not a road is suitable to be driven.

Wildlife

Normally, wild animals flee from humans and therefore present almost no danger at all to hikers. However, javelinas, skunks, raccoons, and other normally harmless critters can become quite defensive if cornered in a small space, such as a room in a prehistoric cliff dwelling. Never enter into an enclosed room, cave, or enclave unless you are sure there are no animals inside. Also check for beehives and wasp nests.

You may also encounter rattlesnakes in and around ruins. I did while hiking to ruins in Devil's Chasm, in Roger's Canyon, and on Skull Mesa, and I no doubt stepped near many others I never even saw. Only a very small percentage of hikers get bitten by rattlesnakes, but be aware that the poisonous creatures are out there.

Use Common Sense

Above all, use common sense when visiting Native American ruins. If a cliff looks tall, stay away from its edge. If the day is late, don't begin a long hike. Take note of mountains and other natural features next to your parked vehicle so you can find your way back after hiking to a ruin, and always let someone at home know exactly where you're going.

ABOUT THE MAPS

The maps in this guidebook were designed to assist in overall preparation and planning for your trip. They are *not* intended to be used as substitutes for topographic or other detailed maps essential to navigation on any backcountry adventure. I highly recommend using a USGS 7.5-minute topographic map on every hike. The quadrangle names of the maps you will need are provided.

Arizona

The Hohokam Culture

The Hohokam culture appeared along the lower Salt and Gila rivers sometime between A.D. 100 and 600. There are many theories about the origins of these people, but the one accepted by most archaeologists today is that the Hohokam evolved from Archaic Indians who had been living in Arizona as far back as 8,000 B.C.

The Salt-Gila basin, which today includes downtown Phoenix, is often called the Hohokam core area because it was the location of the culture's largest and most influential villages. The Hohokam also moved up tributaries of the two rivers, establishing smaller, more distant communities along the Santa Cruz, San Pedro, Verde, Agua Fria, New, and Hassayampa rivers, as well as along Tonto Creek, Queen Creek, and other waterways. These outlying areas are often referred to as the Hohokam periphery or frontier. After being isolated from the core area for centuries, some peripheral communities developed so many unique traits that they became cultures in their own right. The Salado and Verde Hohokam—two prehistoric groups that will be discussed in later chapters—stand out as good examples of Native Americans whose origins can be traced to the people of the Salt-Gila basin.

AGRICULTURE, HUNTING, AND GATHERING

In the Hohokam core area, the Native Americans dug an extensive network of canals that diverted water from the Salt and Gila rivers onto fields of corn, beans, squash, cotton, tobacco, and other crops. The Salt River Valley alone contained more than 700 miles of canals, making it home to the most complex irrigation system in aboriginal North America. A surprisingly high number of the ancient waterways followed the same paths as modern Salt River Project canals, suggesting the Native Americans had considerable knowledge of hydrology.

Communities on the Hohokam periphery also built canals, but irrigation in the outlying areas was usually less important than dry farming, a technique that uses rock piles, diversion dams, terraces, and other devices to capture and divert rainfall and rain runoff onto agricultural fields. While dry farming is generally less sophisticated than irrigation, it was actually more effective in many mountainous areas where canals could not be built easily.

Although highly successful as farmers, the Hohokam supplemented their cultivated diet by gathering mesquite beans, paloverde beans, saguaro fruit, and many other wild plant foods. They also hunted deer, rabbits, bighorn sheep, and other animals.

POTTERY AND OTHER CRAFTS

One of the key traits separating the Hohokam from their Archaic ancestors was the production of pottery. The Hohokam made quite an art of this, decorating their pots and bowls with many beautiful motifs, including their hallmark "red-on-buff" ware, featuring red designs painted over a light, buff-colored surface.

These Native Americans also transformed their cotton into colorful textiles and worked clay and stone into a variety of figurines. They even fashioned bracelets, necklaces, and other jewelry from shells from the Sea of Cortez obtained through trade. The large core-area villages probably dealt directly with the coastal traders, then passed some of the shells on to peripheral communities in exchange for timber, wild foods, or other goods.

FROM PITHOUSES TO PUEBLOS

Early Hohokam villages consisted primarily of partially buried pithouses made from mud and sticks. Often the pithouses were clustered in groups around a central plaza. Many villages also featured large, oval-shaped holes in the ground called ball courts. Some prehistoric Native Americans in Mexico used similar courts to play a game somewhat like soccer, and this has led many researchers to believe the Hohokam used their courts for the same purpose. The Hohokam also may have used ball courts for ceremonies and ritualistic dances, or as meeting places to conduct trade.

Over time the Native Americans learned to build with stone and adobe, and by A.D. 1200 many villages in the Salt-Gila basin boasted above-ground, multistory pueblos made from these materials. High walls often encompassed groups of houses or an entire settlement. The ball courts that characterized earlier villages faded away and were replaced by huge adobe-capped platform mounds. The elite residents in some villages built their homes on top of the giant platforms, and some mounds may have also served as meeting places for ceremonies or political business. Some believe the platform mounds also played a defensive role, providing the Hohokam with protection from hostile outside groups.

With their big buildings and impressive public architecture, the largest core-area villages may have had up to 2,000 residents. The ruins of one village, El Pueblo de los Muertos just south of present-day Tempe, were over 5 miles long before twentieth-century farmers plowed them under.

Villages on the Hohokam periphery never achieved such splendor. Native Americans living on the frontier did, however, build many fascinating structures made of stone at the very tops of hills, mountains, mesas, and buttes. The fortified appearance of the hilltop sites suggests defensive tactics, although archaeologists have proposed many other uses for them. Virtually all of the Hohokam ruins in this book's individual site descriptions fall into the general category of fortified hilltops, and a more thorough discussion of this type of ruin is offered below.

THE DOWNFALL

Despite all the related accomplishments, the Hohokam system began to fall apart in the late 1300s, and by the year 1400 these Native Americans had all but vanished. Many blame their demise on massive floods that occurred during the 1380s. The climatic disaster is said to have wreaked havoc on their farms and canals, leaving them with a stunted economy that in turn created severe social problems. Other theories, some of which incorporate the flooding scenario, emphasize internal strife or conflicts with other cultures. Any of these problems, and perhaps many others, could have combined to destroy the Hohokam.

Although the Hohokam disappeared as a culture, relatively small numbers of them actually may have continued living in Arizona. Many believe the present-day Pima and Tohono O'odham (Papago) tribes are living descendants of the Hohokam. In the Piman language, the word *Hohokam* means "those who have gone" or "all used up."

The Pimas and their cousins are not the only people to have recognized the remnants of those who came before them. The city of Phoenix was named after the Phoenix bird because, like the creature from Greek mythology, the modern city in the desert literally rose to new life from the ashes of a previously great society.

THE HILLTOP RUINS

Every year, thousands of people visit such well-known archaeological ruins as Pueblo Grande in Phoenix and Casa Grande ruins in Coolidge. The attraction is understandable, for the remains of these large core-area villages, along with the museums built next to them, provide fascinating glimpses into the lives of those we call the Hohokam. Few people, however, wander off the beaten path to explore the many undeveloped ruins that dot the outer reaches of the Hohokam region. It is here—beyond the sidewalks, tour guides, and entry fees—where the more adventurous ruin seekers find the hilltop sites.

As mentioned, hilltop ruins are located at the very top of hills, mountains, mesas, and buttes. The remote and rugged terrain surrounding these places often makes access difficult, but for those with a strong appreciation of Native American ruins, the hiking, climbing, and bushwhacking required to reach them is well worth the effort. Hilltop ruins are by no means the only type of archaeological sites on the Hohokam periphery, but they do represent some of the area's most intriguing and best-preserved ruins.

A central question surrounding the hilltop sites is Why so high? Many have suggested the Hohokam built structures on top of hills in order to defend themselves from enemies. Indeed, one has only to look at the fortlike appearance of many hilltop ruins to understand how such theories come about. The cliffs or steep hillsides surrounding the sites would have given the occupants an obvious advantage over attackers. A great wall usually surrounds all the rooms at the summit, making access even more difficult.

The Hohokam built nine rooms of stone at the summit of this mountain near the New River. The ruin, which is surrounded by cliffs and offers a commanding view of the surrounding terrain, is typical of a prehistoric hilltop site.

Such walls often have tiny peepholes, called loopholes, that provide people inside the "forts" with protected views of the village entrance or any other vulnerable spots on the surrounding slopes that could provide access for invaders.

So which Native Americans did the attacking? Many believe warfare involved intraregional conflict. Droughts during the eleventh and twelfth centuries may have caused shortages of food, well-watered land, and other resources. A period of low moisture would have created a particularly desperate situation on the Hohokam periphery because communities there relied heavily on dry farming, which is more vulnerable to drought than irrigation farming. Competition for resources in some of the outlying areas apparently became so fierce that some villages or village alliances resorted to raiding their neighbors.

If Native Americans on the periphery did not clash with their immediate neighbors, they may have fought with villages in the Hohokam core area. It has been proposed that the large communities in the Salt-Gila basin also suffered from periods of drought and perhaps such other forms of environmental deterioration as soil salinity and insect infestation in their fields. These problems reduced their ability to produce enough food and other resources to sustain their large populations. The powerful core-area villages, as the theory goes, responded to hard times by forcing smaller Hohokam settlements located farther from the Salt-Gila basin to pay "tributes" in the form of food, timber, cotton, or other resources. Some of the outlying communities rebelled, instigating conflicts that necessitated the construction of hilltop retreats for defense.

It should be noted, however, that aside from the defensive appearance of many hilltop ruins, there is little evidence that warfare even existed in Hohokam society. Specialized weapons, mutilated skeletons, or petroglyphs depicting scenes of warfare simply don't turn up at many archaeological sites. This may be due in part to the fact that unlike the Vikings, Aztecs, Plains Indians, and other great conquerors of history, Native Americans in the Southwest did not make heroes out of their warriors and therefore did not include pictures of them in their artwork. Also, if warfare did exist, it probably took the form of raiding by relatively small bands who were more interested in stealing resources from their neighbors than killing or conquering them. The Hohokam may have built small forts, but they did not engage in the type of large-scale battles we tend to associate with European castles.

Although defense is the most common explanation for hilltop ruins, several other theories have been developed. Many believe the Native Americans may have placed numerous sites within view of each other in order to create signaling networks that allowed them to quickly communicate over great distances by passing messages from one hilltop to the next. The exact nature of the signals is not known, although fire or smoke seems most likely. Evidence for the signaling theory lies in the fact that the lofty locales can be seen for miles, with a surprisingly high number of hilltop ruins within viewing range of other hilltop ruins, which are in turn within site of additional hilltops. In fact, at one time, it was reportedly possible to make line-of-sight contact from one site to another all the way from the Phoenix area to the south rim of the Grand Canyon.

The hilltop sites also would have made good lookout posts. Often perched on hills, buttes, or mesas adjacent to larger settlements, the sky-high structures would have provided a village watchman with a bird's-eye view of traders, hostile groups, or anyone else approaching an area.

Some of the ruins also appear to have been used as permanent living quarters. The sheer number of rooms at some of the larger pueblos suggests the Native Americans called the hilltops home. The presence of metates and manos—stone troughs with handheld grinding rocks for processing food— and other artifacts at many of the larger ruins provides additional evidence that the sites functioned as regular living quarters.

Most hilltop ruins, however, are relatively small and appear to have been used only temporarily. Perhaps some hilltop sites started out small and temporary, then grew into larger, more permanent settlements over time as the Hohokam encountered a greater need to defend themselves, send signals, or conduct other hilltop activities.

Whatever their purpose, it is not likely that any single theory can explain the role of hilltop ruins. Different hilltop sites may have served different purposes, and any single hilltop may have played a multifunctional role. Hilltops used as forts, for example, may have also served as lookout stations from which to watch for enemies and signal distant villages of approaching danger.

Hilltop ruins are not limited to the Hohokam. They have been built by a variety of prehistoric cultures including the Salado, Verde Hohokam, and Sinagua, and various types of hilltop sites exist throughout the American Southwest and northern Mexico.

1 New River

Type of hike: Bushwhack, out-and-back.
Total distance: About 1 mile.
Difficulty: Moderate.
Topo maps: USGS quads—Daisy Mountain, New River.
Ruin coordinates: N33° 57' 53" W112° 03' 52".
Administration: Tonto National Forest.

If you've never ventured into the desert to see a Hohokam "fortified hilltop" before, this pueblo near the New River would make a good introductory trip because it is so typical of hilltop ruins.

Located at the summit of a rugged, steep-sloped mountain, the ruin has five or six easily recognizable rooms formed with ancient walls of stone. Most of the crumbling old walls only stand 1 or 2 feet high, but one particularly well-preserved room in the center of the pueblo has four chest-high walls that remain unbroken except for a clearly defined entrance. Researchers working on the Central Arizona Ecotone Project, which included surveys and excavations of many archaeological sites in the upper New River area, found that the ruin had a total of nine rooms when it was built sometime between A.D. 800 and 1150.

Cliffs surround much of the ruin, making access difficult and giving the pueblo a fortlike appearance. A thick exterior wall also surrounds parts of the ruin. If you look closely, you'll realize that the wall only exists in areas where there are no cliffs. We are left to wonder why, if the outer wall served a purpose other than defense, the Native Americans built it only in areas not protected by natural barriers.

You can also find a few petroglyphs pecked into the rocks on the south side of the mountain just below the ruin. They're not the best preserved glyphs in the world, but you can make out several abstract designs if you look very hard.

While hiking to the ruin, you may stumble across a second pueblo at the base of the mountain on the north side. The ruin at the base is actually much larger than the ruin at the summit, but it's not nearly as visible because the walls have almost completely disappeared. Archaeologists have speculated that Native Americans living in the larger pueblo may have used

New River

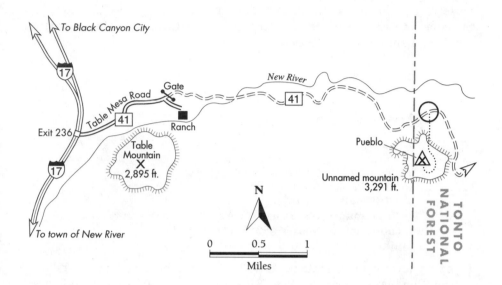

the smaller site at the summit as a temporary retreat during times of conflict.

How to get there: A trip to this ruin requires about 0.5 mile of bushwhacking up a mountain that rises nearly 700 feet from the desert floor. Wear long pants for protection against the brush. Before the hike begins, there is a 4.25-mile drive on a dirt road, the last 2 or 3 miles of which require a high-clearance vehicle.

From the town of New River, drive north on Interstate 17 and take the first exit you encounter, which is Exit 236, onto Table Mesa Road. This road is not paved and is marked on many maps as Forest Road 41. Head east (turning right off the freeway) on FR 41 for about a mile to the entrance of the Vanderwey Ranch (shown on topo maps as the Tee Ranch). Do not turn right into the ranch entrance. Instead, get out of your vehicle, open the gate ahead of you, pass through the fence, and shut the gate behind you so cattle don't wander off their range. Continue driving east on FR 41. You will not be driving on private land. Continue on the dirt road for another 3.25 miles until you reach a cattle guard, a second barbed-wire fence, a small corral, and a sign saying you have just entered Tonto National Forest. There is no designated parking, but there is a clearing near the corral where you can pull off the road and park.

Note that the barbed-wire fence marking the border to Tonto National Forest leads up a hill on the south side of the road and continues up a tall, pointed, unnamed mountain. The ruin is on the very top of that mountain—not *near* the top but *on* the top, at the absolute highest point possible. The distance to the top is about 0.5 mile. To get there, bushwhack up the mountain along the left (east) side of the barbed-wire fence. This will get you

The best-preserved room in the New River ruin features four chest-high walls and a clearly defined entrance.

close to the summit, but the final ascent must be made from the south side of the mountain. Swing around to the south side and scramble up the rocks to reach the peak and all the ruins.

2 Indian Mesa

Type of hike: Day hike with some bushwhacking, out-and-back.
Total distance: About 5 miles.
Difficulty: Moderate.
Topo map: USGS quad—New River.
Ruin coordinates: N33° 57' 54" W112° 13' 37".
Administration: Bureau of Land Management.

The prehistoric ruin on Indian Mesa has an appearance not unlike Masada, an ancient fortress near the Dead Sea where a group of Jewish zealots found protection from Roman soldiers. Like the Jewish stronghold, the Hohokam ruin is perched atop a mountain and surrounded by cliffs. Also like Masada, Indian Mesa is located at the shore of a large body of water, in this case Lake Pleasant.

Strictly speaking, cliffs do not surround the entire ruin. You can access the mesa top relatively easily from one small area. The Hohokam

Indian Mesa

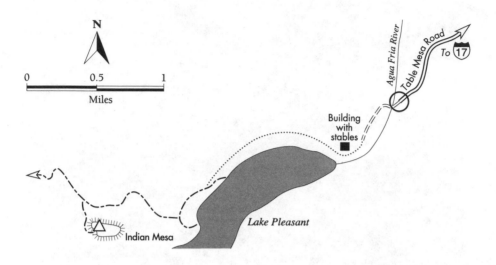

concentrated a great deal of their wall-building efforts near the entrance, apparently to add more protection to the pueblo's most vulnerable spot. These walls, which are several feet high and about 3 feet thick, contain numerous loopholes that enabled occupants to see who was approaching the village gate. The Hohokam probably created the little windows strictly for visual purposes, but one can't help imagining people shooting arrows through them.

Of course, modern "invaders" have relatively little trouble penetrating the village, and once past the entrance you'll find about a dozen rooms with walls still intact. One particularly well-preserved room in the center of the mesa has four bleach-white walls of rock and mud that in some areas stand more than 5 feet high. Researchers who surveyed the ruin for the Central Arizona Ecotone Project found that the site had at least 16 rooms when it was built sometime between A.D. 800 and 1150.

At the west end of the mesa you'll also find a small, perfectly round hole bored into the rock floor. This may be a mortar hole.

Lake Pleasant is a modern development. However, the Agua Fria River, which feeds the lake, has always existed at the base of Indian Mesa and no doubt is the water source that attracted the Hohokam to the area.

How to get there: The easiest way to reach this ruin is to hop in a boat at one of the launch ramps at the south end of Lake Pleasant, then zip across the water to the base of Indian Mesa, which is located just west of the mouth of the Agua Fria River. Most people, however, will drive 5 miles on a well-graded dirt road before embarking on a 2.5-mile hike (one way) that includes some serious bushwhacking. The last 0.75 mile of the hike rises about 400 feet.

If you are beginning the trip from Phoenix with only a car and a pair of hiking boots, drive north on Interstate 17. Pass the town of New River, then take Exit 236 (Table Mesa Road). Turn left, crossing over I-17, then immediately right onto the highway frontage road. Heading north, the paved frontage road parallels I-17 for a bit, then becomes Table Mesa Road and veers left (west) away from the highway. Stay on Table Mesa, which is the main dirt road, and the widest, best-maintained one, for 5 miles until you reach the Agua Fria River. When you reach the river, evaluate the water level carefully. If it's not too high and you have a high-clearance vehicle, you can cross the river and continue on the road about 0.25 mile or so to an old building with some stables. Park there. If you don't want to drive across the Agua Fria, park at the river, cross the water, and hike to the building.

The road you are on used to lead right up to the base of Indian Mesa. Today, it is blocked by the old building. It also takes a major dip into Lake Pleasant, which had a dramatic increase in water level in 1993 (the lake crept up the Agua Fria almost to the building). The objective, then, is to get around both the building and the lake. Getting around the building is easy. Just walk around it along the riverbed to the left and pick up the road on the other side of all the stables. Getting around the lake is a different story. When the road hits the water, you must turn right and bushwhack over difficult terrain around the perimeter of the lake until you reach the point where the road comes back out of the water. The terrain around the lake is steep and heavily overgrown with shirt-grabbing brush, so the bushwhacking will require the bulk of your hiking time.

Once you get around the lake, continue on the road. It will soon fork. Take the road to the right and walk another 0.75 mile to the base of Indian Mesa, which will be on your left. There is also a smaller mountain just west of the big mesa with a trail leading up it. Follow the trail up the smaller, unnamed mountain, then to the saddle between the smaller mountain and Indian Mesa. From there, the trail swings around to the southwest side of Indian Mesa and right up to the entrance to the ruin. If you find yourself doing some serious rock climbing to get on top of the mesa, you have not followed the trail far enough. Again, the trail leads right up to an easy entrance on the southwest side of Indian Mesa.

Indian Mesa is close, but not within the boundaries of Lake Pleasant Regional Park. If your map predates 1989, it may show Indian Mesa as being on Arizona State Trust land.

3 Hieroglyphic Canyon

Type of hike:	Day hike, out-and-back.
Total distance:	About 3.5 miles.
Difficulty:	Easy.
Topo map:	USGS quad—Goldfield.
Ruin coordinates:	N33° 24' 29" W111° 25' 08".
Administration:	Tonto National Forest.

One look at Hieroglyphic Canyon and you can tell the place was once prime mountain sheep habitat. The cliffs surrounding this rugged gorge in the Superstition Mountains look tailor-made for surefooted desert bighorns, and the lush vegetation at the bottom of the canyon would have provided plenty of food. There is even a bubbling spring in the lower part of the canyon that produces more water than an entire herd could drink. The only question is What happened to all the sheep?

The answer is that the local sheep population was wiped out in the early 1900s by overhunting, habitat encroachment by miners, stress from recreationists, and other factors associated with settling the area. It is sad that the animals no longer inhabit the canyon, but their story makes for some thought-provoking petroglyphs. If you hike to the spring, you'll find large stone panels covered with pictures of sheep that now serve as prehistoric fossils of the locally extinct species. One scene shows eight sheep walking in a line, and another appears to depict a ewe giving birth. Most of the sheep, however, look like they're simply hanging out on the rocks, as bighorns often do.

Donald E. Weaver Jr., an archaeologist who investigated the site, speculates that the Hohokam hunted sheep for food and also placed some sort of religious or spiritual importance on them. Sometime between A.D. 900 and 1100, Native Americans using Hieroglyphic Canyon as a base camp for hunting and gathering became concerned that the sheep population was dwindling, possibly due to excessive hunting by several different tribes in the area. To ensure the continued availability of the sheep, the Hohokam sought spiritual assistance and conducted some sort of ritual or activity that included drawing sheep on the rocks. The spring was a natural location for this artwork because the sheep regularly gathered around the waterhole to drink.

The Native Americans' efforts apparently worked, for sheep continued to live in the canyon long after the Hohokam stopped hunting in the area. In fact, the animals hung on for another 800 years or so until European-Americans began to change things. However, don't get the idea that all twentieth-century Arizonans had it in for the sheep. Just like the Hohokam, modern wildlife biologists have been concerned with the vanishing sheep population. They even made several attempts in the 1960s and 1970s to reintroduce bighorns into the western part of the Superstitions. However, after being turned loose, the animals wandered away into other parts of the range.

Hieroglyphic Canyon

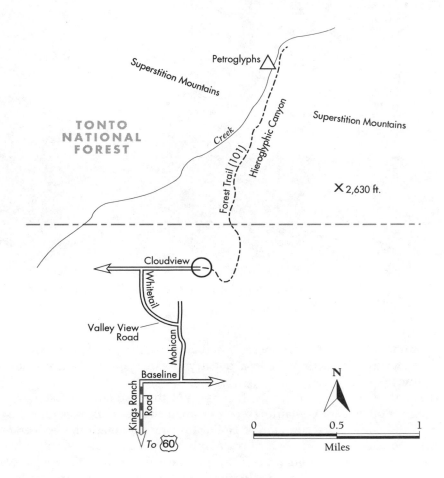

When you get tired of counting sheep, you can observe a variety of other petroglyphs around the spring in Hieroglyphic Canyon. There are almost as many deer as there are desert bighorns, and their interpretation is more or less the same as for the sheep. You'll also see a striking image of a stick figure wearing a headdress, plus a wide array of geometric patterns and designs.

One of the more prominent designs is that of a spiral, an image that shows up at many Hohokam rock art sites and has received a wide range of interpretations. One of the more interesting theories about spirals maintains that they function as solstice markers. For example, at Petrified Forest National Park in northeastern Arizona, a crooked shadow line moves across a particular spiral petroglyph as the sun rises on the first day of summer. When the crooked line bisects the center of the spiral, it becomes a straight line. Some spirals also mark the arrival of the winter solstice, vernal equinox,

Drawings of bighorn sheep are common in Hieroglyphic Canyon. This fading petroglyph panel includes eight sheep walking in a line.

or autumnal equinox. I cannot say whether or not the spiral in Hieroglyphic Canyon interacts with a shadow, but if you show up during a solstice or equinox you may find out.

Another prominent petroglyph consists of three squares stacked on top of one another, each containing a pair of small circles. This image is called a "pipette" and is very common at Hohokam sites, although the appearance tends to vary a bit from one site to another. Pipettes bear a strong resemblance to rock art in southern New Mexico depicting Tlaloc, the goggle-eyed rain god of Mesoamerica, and the similarities have led some experts to believe that Hohokam pipettes may also represent some sort of deity.

If you are taking photographs, be sure to bring a telephoto lens because many of the petroglyphs are too high up on the rocks to frame tightly with a regular lens.

How to get there: This trip includes about 1.8 miles of hiking (one way) on a well-established trail and 1.5 miles of driving on well-graded dirt roads.

From Apache Junction, 30 miles east of Phoenix, head east on U.S. Highway 60 (toward Florence Junction) for 7 miles to Kings Ranch Road. Turn left on Kings Ranch Road and continue for about 3 miles until the pavement ends. For the next 1.5 miles or so, follow the dirt roads, turning right on Baseline, left on Mohican, left on Valley View, right on Whitetail, and right on Cloudview. At the end of Cloudview, you'll find a parking area and the head of Trail 101. The trailhead is not marked, so you might have to get out of your car to see it.

Follow Trail 101 east for 0.25 mile or so, then north toward the Superstition Mountains and into Hieroglyphic Canyon. After turning north and hiking another 1.5 miles, you'll see the very prominent petroglyphs on the left side of the trail, where the trail actually goes down to the creek at the bottom of Hieroglyphic Canyon. This is the main petroglyph site, but you can find more rock art if you hike down the creek 100 yards or so.

4 Gila Bend

Type of hike:	Bushwhack, out-and-back.
Total distance:	About 3.5 miles.
Difficulty:	Moderate.
Topo maps:	USGS quads—Citrus Valley East, Smurr.
Ruin coordinates:	N33° 00' 17" W112° 45' 30".
Administration:	Archaeological site owned by Tohono O'odham Nation, surrounded by land administered by the Bureau of Land Management.

If you really want to see what a Hohokam fortified hilltop looked like before centuries of wind, rain, and gravity reduced it to rubble, take a hike to the ruin located just across the Gila River from the town of Gila Bend. The rooms of this place appear so intact you're likely to question whether or not you're actually wandering among prehistoric buildings.

The ruin has more than forty rock rooms, all clustered in groups on top of an isolated mesa in the desert. Some of the walls stand as high as 7 feet. Only the roofs, which were probably made of mud and thatch supported by wooden beams, appear to be missing from the buildings. Some of the rooms are thought to have served as permanent living quarters, others for storage or ceremonial purposes.

The site also has a great rock wall, 125 paces in length, that bisects the slanted mesa top in the center and divides the village into an upper and lower ruin. One archaeologist suggested that Native Americans living in the lower village might have retreated to the high side of the big wall when under attack.

Mortar holes are found all over this ruin, especially in the bedrock at the very tip of the mesa.

Before you get too excited about this place, there's something you should know. The ruin was excavated in the 1960s, and the crew that conducted the dig also reconstructed forty-three of the pueblo's fifty-seven original rooms. The majority of those "well-preserved" walls were rebuilt by modern workers. This was done in anticipation of the establishment of a public park, although it's hard to understand why anyone would rather see a

Gila Bend

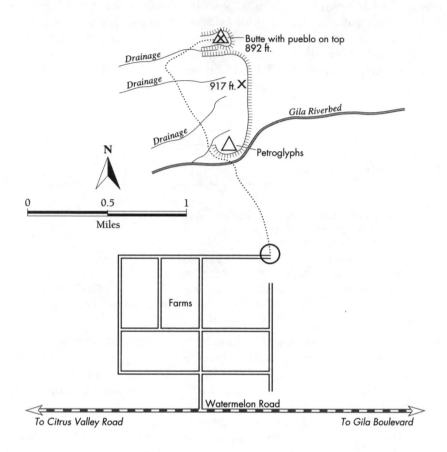

reconstructed village than a fully authentic Native American ruin, even if it's crumbling to the ground. The public park never came to be. In fact, the only good road leading to the ruin was completely washed out when the Gila River flooded in 1993, leaving the site isolated from any member of the public unwilling to trek through a lot of very rugged terrain to reach it.

The excavation did, however, provide some interesting insights into the lives of those who lived in the village. J. Cameron Greenleaf, an archaeologist who assisted with the excavation, wrote that the site's architecture, pottery, and burials strongly resembled those of Native Americans who lived in the Tucson basin during roughly the same time. The similarities led Greenleaf to conclude that the village was built by a group of related families who migrated from the Tucson area to the Gila Bend area around A.D. 1200 and constructed the village over a period of about seventy-five years, adding more rooms from time to time. The defensive nature of the ruin provided the migrants with assurance that they would be safe from attacks, possibly from forerunners of Yuma Indians who lived farther down the Gila River.

While hiking to this ruin, you may wonder how the Native Americans managed to survive in such a dry and desolate place. There is no doubt that life was hard in the thirteenth century, but the area was not as dry as you might think. Captain Juan Mateo Manje, who saw the "Jila River" in 1697 while traveling with the Jesuit missionary Father Eusebio Francisco Kino, wrote that it looked possible to navigate the waterway in a ship. Additionally, while excavating the ruin archaeologists found, among many other things, the vertebrae of a Colorado squawfish. This species lived in the Gila River and could grow as heavy as 90 pounds. A river with enough water to support ships and 90-pound fish most certainly provided enough water to grow corn, beans, and squash; indeed, many prehistoric farms and canals have been located in the Gila Bend area.

After visiting the ruin, you may want to hike over to the southwest end of the mesa to see a nice display of petroglyphs. One of the glyphs shows several deer or bighorn sheep involved in some crazy activity in which they're all floating around in the air and grabbing each other's tails.

Another petroglyph looks exactly like a sunflower. The image is strikingly similar to another "sunflower" pecked onto a rock at the Sears Point petroglyph site, located roughly 30 miles down the Gila River. The "flower" at Sears Point actually represents the sun, and one researcher found that if you stand near the glyph during the summer solstice, you can watch the real sun set into a large nook on the horizon. It would be interesting to see if the "sunflower" petroglyph at the Gila Bend ruin also marks a place to observe the solstice.

This book names ruins according to their location, but many people call the site near Gila Bend the "Fortified Hill," and sometimes the near Spanish equivalent, *Fortaleza*.

The Tohono O'odham Nation owns this site and does not allow photography, so don't bother bringing a camera.

How to get there: The desert surrounding this ruin is administered by the Bureau of Land Management. However, the archaeological site itself is owned by the Tohono O'odham Nation, and you must obtain a permit from this tribe to actually walk among the prehistoric buildings. To get a permit, stop by the San Lucy Village District Office in Gila Bend and tell the people there where you want to go. Bring a picture ID and be prepared to briefly explain your reason for visiting the site. The permit is free, and if your intentions are sound you should be in and out of the office in about ten minutes.

The district office is at 1216 307th Avenue. From Pima Street, the main strip in Gila Bend, drive north on St. Louis Avenue. Take a left when you reach Indian Road, then turn right on 307th Avenue. The office will be down the road a bit, on the left. It's not open on weekends, but the permits are good for several days, so you can pick one up during the week and use it on the following Saturday or Sunday. Also, you may want to call the office before you go to make sure the district council chairperson will be in when you arrive, for she must sign your permit. The phone number is (520) 683-6515.

With permit in hand, you are ready to head to the ruin. The following suggested route requires a very short drive on well-graded dirt roads followed by about 1.75 miles (one way) of heavy-duty bushwhacking. You'll want long sleeves and long pants for protection against the brush. A compass may come in handy for navigating through the dense vegetation.

To reach the ruin from Gila Bend, head north on Gila Boulevard. The boulevard is not marked, but it begins just west of McDonald's on Pima Street. Drive about 2 miles on Gila, then take a left on Watermelon Road. Follow Watermelon about 1.5 miles to a dirt road that turns right onto some farmland. Continue north on the dirt road as far as you can. At this point, you should be able to look north and see the butte on which the ruin sits. If you have binoculars or good vision, you may be able to see some of the walls of the ruin. Now, turn right (east), continue on the dirt road as far as you can (about 0.5 mile), and park off to the side of the road.

There used to be a dirt road that led from the general area where you now stand all the way to the base of the butte (you can still see it on old USGS topo maps). The road no longer exists, so you're going to have to bushwhack about 1.75 miles to reach the ruin. The trek will take you across the usually dry Gila River and through some very thick brush. There is no best route, but you'll find a network of trails stomped through the brush by either people or animals that can make the going easier. If a trail you happen to be following suddenly stops or veers off in the wrong direction, continue through the brush until you pick up another one.

It's very easy to get disoriented in this mess of trails and brush, so if your natural sense of direction is poor, use a compass. From anywhere in the brush, if you head north you'll eventually reach the butte, and if you head south you'll eventually return to the farms and dirt roads.

When you reach the butte, you'll discover that it actually consists of a series of small buttes separated by small canyons or drainages. The ruin is located on top of the northernmost butte, the one farthest from where you parked. Cliffs will prevent you from climbing the butte from any direction but west. The 230-foot climb is not too difficult.

As mentioned, the petroglyphs are located at the southernmost tip of the buttes (an area shown on USGS topo maps as the Point of Rocks). In order to see them, you must climb up on the rocks a bit. None of this scrambling is difficult. The artwork is spread out quite a bit, so look all around the area.

5   Gila Bend Mountains

Type of hike:	Bushwhack, out-and-back.
Total distance:	About 3 miles.
Difficulty:	Moderate.
Topo maps:	USGS quads—Cotton Center, Gila Bend.
Ruin coordinates:	N33° 00' 17" W112° 43' 11".
Administration:	Archaeological site owned by Tohono O'odham Nation, surrounded by land administered by the Bureau of Land Management.

If you liked the petroglyphs at the Gila Bend ruin, you might want to trek to a second site located a few miles to the east, at the base of the Gila Bend Mountains. It's a difficult place to reach, but all the rock art in the area makes the trip well worth the effort.

Pictures of stick people are everywhere at this site. One of the people sports a long, wavy headdress. Other stick people have solid circles in the middle of their bodies. Archaeologists have noted similar petroglyphs at Painted Rock State Park about 15 miles downriver but have not been able to determine if the solid circles represent garments or body elaborations. Still other stick people have "tails" between their legs, which are often interpreted as male phalli. One obvious guess as to the meaning of the solid circles would be that they depict pregnancy, but many of the glyphs have both circles and phalli, which mystifies this theory.

Other drawings include an impressive lizard and a variety of simple four-legged animals that might be deer, bighorn sheep, coyotes, or all of these animals. You'll also see a lot of abstract markings like grids, ladders, circles, spirals, bull's eyes, zigzag lines, and an image resembling a swastika. Of course, what we see as abstract might have represented something very real to the Native Americans who made the glyphs. At other petroglyph sites, for example, zigzags have been interpreted as snakes and sometimes falling rain.

In the 1960s, the archaeologists William W. Wasley and Alfred E. Johnson surveyed these petroglyphs. They also found decorated pottery at some nearby Hohokam villages that featured the same designs they had seen at the petroglyph site. This led them to conclude that the Hohokam probably made most of the rock art as well.

Photography is prohibited at this archaeological site in the Gila Bend Mountains.

How to get there: This site, like the ruin in the previous chapter, is surrounded by BLM land. However, the petroglyph site itself is owned by the Tohono O'odham Nation so you must get a permit from this tribe to actually walk among the rock art. See the "How to Get There" section of the previous chapter for instructions on how to obtain a permit.

As mentioned, this trip includes 1.5 miles (one way) of pretty severe bushwhacking, so wear long pants and long sleeves for protection against

Gila Bend Mountains

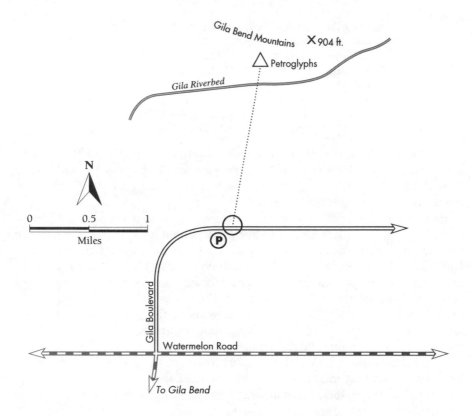

brush. Before the hike, a very short drive follows a well-graded dirt road. A compass might come in handy for navigation.

From the town of Gila Bend, head north on Gila Boulevard. The boulevard is not marked, but it begins just west of McDonald's on Pima Street, the town's main strip. Drive about 2 miles on Gila, then continue straight across Watermelon Road and onto a dirt road. Follow the dirt road for about 1.5 miles as it curves to the right (east), then park somewhere along the side of the road shortly after you make the curve.

From where you parked, you will be able to see the Gila Bend Mountains about 1.5 miles to the north. Note that the extreme right (east) end of the range comes down to a point as it meets the desert floor. The petroglyphs are located at the base of the mountains about 0.5 mile left (west) of that point. There is no best route to the glyphs. Just push your way across the pathless Gila Riverbed, through the thick brush and on to the mountains.

When you reach the petroglyphs, take some time to explore the place thoroughly. Most of the rock art is concentrated on a single pile of dark boulders, but you'll find more if you wander up the mountain about 0.25 mile east of the main site.

6 Picacho Mountains

Type of hike: Drive-up.
Total distance: None.
Difficulty: Easy.
Topo map: USGS quad—Picacho Reservoir (dirt roads not shown on topo map).
Petroglyph coordinates: Largest site at N32° 50' 03" W111° 23' 01".
Administration: Arizona State Land Department.

If you've ever driven Interstate 10 between Phoenix and Tucson, you've seen that towering icon in the desert known as Picacho Peak. What you probably have not seen are the massive concentrations of petroglyphs that can be found after turning off the pavement and heading into lesser known parts of the Picacho Mountains.

Archaeologists have recorded more than 4,000 petroglyphs in the Picachos. The drawings appear in clusters at nineteen different sites, with some of the most spectacular displays at the north end of the range, which is on the side of the highway opposite Picacho Peak.

At the largest site, stick-man petroglyphs are everywhere. Many of these depict people with their legs apart and their hands raised in the air, and some depict people with hollow circles in the middle of their bodies. Simple pictures of deer and bighorn sheep also appear here and there, looking more like they were drawn by children than by adults. Other images include suns, circles, four-pointed stars, swastikas, grids, something that looks like a garden rake, and all kinds of squiggly lines that appear to follow no pattern at all.

Henry D. Wallace and James P. Holmund, archaeologists who surveyed all the rock art in the Picachos, noted that some of the deer and sheep were drawn upside down next to the stick people who have their arms upraised. This led them to believe the people might represent hunters and the inverted animals their kill. Rakes and grids may also be related to hunting, perhaps depicting nets or traps used to divert and capture game.

The people with hollow circles in their bodies hint at the concept of pregnancy or fertility, while people lying horizontally or upside down possibly represent illness or death. As for the squiggly lines, many of the glyphs that appear abstract to modern observers may have had a more representational meaning to those who made them. For example, one seemingly meaningless scribble actually outlines the exact shape of a nearby mountain as viewed from above, suggesting that the petroglyph functioned as a map.

The four-pointed stars, sometimes described as outlined crosses, have prompted a variety of interpretations from various researchers. One of the most popular is that the image represents Venus or the morning star. This is not surprising, considering that Venus is popular in folk astronomies all over the world.

Another theory about the star glyphs maintains that they function as

Picacho Mountains

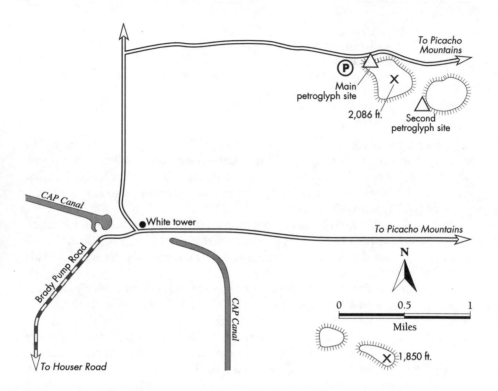

solstice markers. In southern Nevada, a shadow moves across a particular star-shaped petroglyph on the first day of summer; this particular pattern only occurs once a year. A similar event occurs during the winter solstice on a star glyph in Arizona's Petrified Forest. By letting the Native Americans know when the solstice arrived, these stars helped them determine when to plant or harvest crops. I cannot confirm that any petroglyphs in the Picachos function as solstice markers, but some of them might have.

To find a possible meaning for the swastika, one might look to similar petroglyphs made by the Hopi Indians. In that culture, the symbol represents migrations. The center of the swastika marks the center of the universe—which to the Hopis was the American Southwest—and the four extending arms represent migrations in the four directions to populate the earth. The swastika was also a symbol of peace and friendship.

It would be convenient to refer to all the petroglyphs in the Picachos as Hohokam rock art, but the issue of cultural identity is more complicated than that. Wallace and Holmund determined the petroglyphs were drawn by three different groups of Native Americans. Some were drawn by Native Americans from the Archaic period who lived in the Picachos sometime between 8,000 B.C. and A.D. 400. Most of the Archaic glyphs are very faint,

This bighorn sheep petroglyph was originally made by the Hohokam, then repecked by the Pimas or some other protohistoric Native Americans.

and some can hardly be seen at all. Later, during the twelfth and thirteenth centuries, Hohokam Indians pecked more designs onto the rocks. The Hohokam drawings are much easier to see and make up the vast majority of the petroglyphs. Then, sometime between the collapse of the Hohokam culture in the fifteenth century and the arrival of Europeans in the sixteenth century, the Pimas or another group of protohistoric Native Americans actually retraced some of the petroglyphs left by the Hohokam. If you find a strikingly "well-preserved" drawing, chances are it's a Hohokam petroglyph repecked by subsequent groups.

How to get there: This trip requires at least 3.25 miles of driving on some fairly well-graded dirt roads. You wouldn't want to take a lowrider into this neck of the woods, but any vehicle with a moderate amount of ground clearance should be adequate.

The petroglyphs are located on Arizona State Trust land. Many people assume such land is in the public domain and therefore hikers are free to come and go at will. This is not true, and technically you must have a recreational permit from the State Land Department to enter the area. To get a permit, call the department at (602) 524-4631.

To reach the petroglyphs from Interstate 10, get off I-10 at Exit 211, just east of Eloy. Jump onto Arizona 87 and drive north, toward Florence and go 4.0 miles to Houser Road. Turn right on Houser and continue another 5.5 miles to Brady Pump Road. Take a left, and after driving 2.0 miles on Brady, the pavement will end. Major landmarks at this point will be the Central Arizona Project Canal and a tall white tower associated with the canal. Veer right onto the dirt road and continue to the tower. When you reach the tower, the road will fork. Do not take the road to the right that heads east into the mountains. Instead, veer left and take the road that continues north. Drive 1.25 miles until you reach a T-shaped intersection. Turn right, toward the mountains, and continue for 1.75 miles until you reach the edge of the Picacho Mountains.

The first petroglyph site will be on the right side of the road, on a huge pile of dark boulders that completely covers the west side of the very first hill you reach. You'll find a clearing on the ground near the glyphs that serves as a nice parking space. This is the best petroglyph site in the Picachos, but if you want to see more rock art, you can drive or walk to the opposite side of that first big hill to a second good site. The second site is actually located on the west slope of the next mountain to the east, not on the same hill as the first petroglyph site.

If you want to see even more petroglyphs, you'll have to find them yourself. The Native Americans could only make good petroglyphs on dark, heavily patinated rocks, so your chances of finding more sites are pretty good if you drive around on the dirt roads and check all the mountain points covered with black boulders. You may need a high-clearance vehicle, or a pair of hiking boots, in some of the more remote areas.

7 Black Mesa

Type of hike:	Bushwhack, out-and-back.
Total distance:	About 1.5 miles.
Difficulty:	Strenuous.
Topo map:	USGS quad—Black Canyon City.
Ruin coordinates:	N34° 06' 14" W112° 07' 54".
Administration:	Bureau of Land Management.

When you first see Black Mesa, a tall "mountain" just north of Black Canyon City, the idea of climbing to the top seems about as ambitious as climbing Squaw Peak in Phoenix without following the hiking trail. It's a difficult trek, but the ruin at the summit has the best-preserved rooms and the tallest walls of any unreconstructed hilltop site in this book.

The fortlike pueblo had thirteen rooms when it was built by the Hohokam sometime between A.D. 800 and 1150, according to Central Arizona Ecotone Project researchers who surveyed the site. When you visit the ruin, you'll be pleased to find that nearly all the rooms remain basically intact. You're sure to be awed by a great wall surrounding the site that in some areas reaches 12 feet in height.

Two of the rooms on the east side of the ruin have loopholes about a foot

Black Mesa

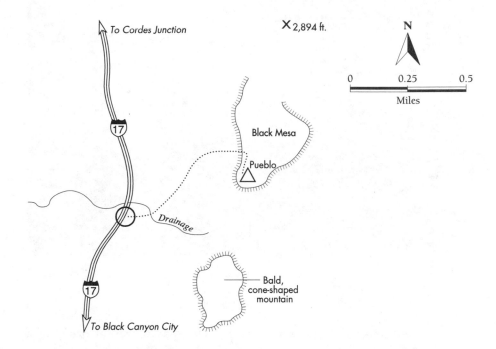

To Cordes Junction

✗ 2,894 ft.

N

0   0.25   0.5

Miles

17

Black Mesa

Pueblo

Drainage

17

To Black Canyon City

Bald,
cone-shaped
mountain

above the ground. Another loophole exists near the pueblo's entrance at the northwest corner, and there are no doubt several others around the site. Much of the ruin is surrounded by cliffs. However, if you look through the loopholes, you'll discover they all enable you to see vulnerable areas around the site where visitors or attackers might have approached.

Perhaps the most remarkable feature of the pueblo is the sheer quantity of rocks used to construct all the walls. The amount of labor required to carry and place so many stones is hard to fathom. No mud or adobe holds the rocks together, so the engineering and craftsmanship required to pile them into stable 12-foot walls are equally impressive. You can't help but wonder how long it took the Hohokam to build this place. One archaeologist who studied over a mile of defensive-type rock walls on top of Tumamoc Hill in the Tucson Mountains believes a hundred people could have built them in about a week. If that's true, maybe the stone pueblo on Black Mesa didn't take nearly as long as you might think.

Black Mesa also has a smattering of petroglyphs pecked onto boulders just outside the ruin on the east side. Most of the drawings are abstractions, although some depict humans and animals. One of the more interesting glyphs looks like a person with arms and legs stretched out, but a long "tail" between the legs suggests it might actually be a lizard. Other notable petroglyphs include several drawings that look a lot like human footprints.

The ruin on Black Mesa has exceptionally tall walls. A loophole is located in the wall of this room about a foot above the ground.

However, each foot has only four toes, so they may represent prints of a large animal.

One thing you will not find at this site is a lot of pottery. That is not to say, however, that there never was any. J. Scott Wood, Forest Archaeologist for Tonto National Forest, claims that when he first saw this ruin in 1963, it was "hip deep" in potsherds. By the time the Central Arizona Ecotone Project researchers surveyed the place in the 1970s, it was reduced to a few mere handfuls. Today, you'd be lucky to find any pottery at all, but if you do, remember that as the years go by, a little theft here and a little theft there can add up to a whole lot of nothing.

After seeing the ruin, walk around on top of the flat, grass-covered mesa. It's a virtual island in the sky with great views in all directions. To the west the Bradshaw Mountains rise high above the desert floor, and to the east the Agua Fria River flows through a great canyon. To the south lies Black Canyon City, a very small town with a disproportionately large dog track.

How to get there: The hike up to the ruin on Black Mesa is less than a mile (one way), but the 750-foot climb is so steep and rugged that you'll need about forty-five minutes and a couple of quarts of drinking water to complete it. Wear long pants for protection against the brush. The only driving on this trip will be on the highway.

Black Mesa is a very common place name in Arizona, and at least two other Black Mesas have Native American ruins associated with them. The subject of this description is located just north of Black Canyon City and just east of Interstate 17.

To reach the ruin from Black Canyon City, drive north on I-17. Start watching the mile markers immediately after leaving the city. Somewhere between mile marker 245 and 246, pull completely off the pavement and park. There are a couple of dirt clearings alongside the highway where this is possible.

The ruin is at the extreme southwest tip of the tall mesa located about a half mile to the northeast of where you parked. For reference, there is a cone-shaped butte directly south of the mesa that looks as if a bulldozer scraped away all its vegetation. There is also a drainage separating Black Mesa from the cone-shaped mountain. No trail leads up to the ruin. Simply scope out what you perceive to be the easiest route up the mountain and bushwhack your way to the top. While plotting a course, note that the southern end of the mesa, where the ruin sits, is surrounded by cliffs. You may want to climb up the less rugged slopes a bit north of the ruin, then walk south to the pueblo once you get on top of the mesa. If you do this, the hiking distance (one way) should be about 0.75 mile.

8 Waterfall Canyon

> **Type of hike:** Day hike with optional bushwhacking, out-and-back.
> **Total distance:** About 2 miles.
> **Difficulty:** Easy up to waterfall (first mile), strenuous beyond that.
> **Topo map:** USGS quad—White Tank Mountains.
> **Rock art coordinates:** Waterfall at N33° 35' 05" W112° 31' 16".
> **Administration:** Maricopa County.

You won't find any prehistoric pueblos or cliff dwellings in Waterfall Canyon, but this cactus-covered patch of desert in the White Tank Mountains contains enough ancient rock art to make it a worthwhile destination.

The trail leading into Waterfall Canyon passes through the site of a village that, according to a 1963 report by archaeologist Alfred E. Johnson, covered 75 acres when it was occupied by the Hohokam between A.D. 500 and 900. No walls or other major features of the village have survived to this day, but all along the trail you can see boulders covered with petroglyphs.

One of the more impressive petroglyph panels, located on a large rock on the north side of the trail only ten minutes into the hike, includes a sun, a stick figure, something resembling a garden rake, an image formed by two perpendicular zigzag lines and other drawings. The sun and stick figure seem straightforward, but one can only guess what the other pictures represent. The rake design appears at many petroglyph sites, and some archaeologists believe it may represent a net or fence used to divert and capture

Waterfall Canyon

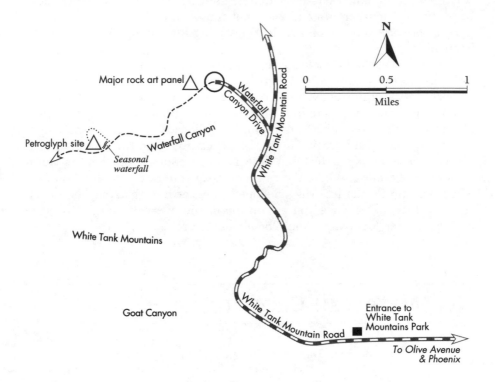

game. The zigzag lines, located immediately left of the rake, may represent snakes or, perhaps, squash vines.

Most people see only the petroglyphs along the first mile of the trail, but you can actually find a much more impressive display just above the falls at the end of the canyon. Getting there is rather difficult, but well worth the steep and rugged climb. All around a pool above the falls, you'll see entire rock walls decorated with stick figures, simple four-legged animals, and a wide array of designs including circles, spirals, grids, and swastikas.

One particularly striking design above the falls consists of a series of rectangles stacked on top of each other, with each rectangle containing two small crosses. This common image is called a "pipette," although most pipettes contain a pair of eyelike circles inside each rectangle, not a pair of crosses. See the site description of Hieroglyphic Canyon for an interpretation of pipettes.

If you explore other areas in the White Tank Mountains in addition to Waterfall Canyon, you may discover petroglyphs made by Archaic and Yavapai Indians as well as the Hohokam.

How to get there: There are no dirt roads on this trip, and if the first mile of the trail leading into Waterfall Canyon was maintained better, it would be a sidewalk—it's wide, flat, and lined with large rocks. However, as mentioned, the climb to get above the falls after the first mile is very steep and rocky.

To reach Waterfall Canyon, drive west on Dunlap Road in North Central Phoenix. Dunlap Road eventually becomes Olive Avenue. Continue west on Olive, past all the farms, to the entrance to White Tank Mountains Regional Park. The entrance to the park is 22 miles from Dunlap and Interstate 17 in Phoenix or about 20 miles from where Dunlap becomes Olive. Someone is usually posted at the entrance, and there is a small entrance fee. Once inside the park, follow White Tank Mountain Road for about 2 miles until you reach Waterfall Canyon Drive, which turns left toward the trailhead at Waterfall Canyon. Park at the trailhead and start walking into the mountains. The petroglyphs will be all around you all along the trail.

If you want to see the rock art above the falls, do *not* continue on the main trail, which goes around the falls on the left (south) side of the canyon. Although more popular, that route does not provide easy access to the petroglyphs once you get above the falls. Instead, look for a poorly maintained "trail" (a route, really) that branches off from the main trail about 100 yards downstream from the falls. It heads straight up the mountain on the north side of the falls. This route is steep and rugged and requires a bit of rock climbing at the top. When you reach the top of the ridge, hike down the other side back toward the waterfall. When you get to the creek, you'll find a large seasonal pool surrounded by an elaborate display of rock art.

This petroglyph panel near the head of the Waterfall Canyon Trail includes a sun, a rake, zigzag lines, and at least one stick figure.

The Verde Hohokam
(Southern Sinagua) Culture

This is the story of a prehistoric people who lived in the Verde Valley of central Arizona. However, before we can discuss them in detail, we must decide what to call them.

For decades this culture was viewed as a group of Sinagua Indians from the Flagstaff area who migrated south during the twelfth century and took up residence in the Verde Valley. Once there, the group encountered Hohokam Indians from the Phoenix basin who had occupied the area for centuries. The newcomers, as the story goes, forced the Hohokam out of the valley or assimilated into Hohokam society to such an extent that the Sinagua became the dominant culture. This popular scenario led to the term "Southern Sinagua," a name that has stuck pretty hard on the people of the Verde Valley.

More recent thinking tends to dispute the theory that the Verde Valley experienced an intrusion from the north. Instead, the existing Hohokam may have instigated many changes on their own during the twelfth century that made them look a lot like the Sinagua. A simple shift in trade relationships, for example, could have resulted in the valley residents acquiring more pottery and other goods from the north than from the south, causing these people to leave behind artifacts that today make them look more like the Sinagua than the Hohokam. Since many experts today believe these Native Americans were indeed a regional variation of the Hohokam, we will consider the term "Southern Sinagua" to be a misnomer and from this point on refer to the people of the Verde Valley as the "Verde Hohokam."

These Native Americans comprised one of the more diverse prehistoric southwestern cultures. Like many other ancient Arizonans, they used canal irrigation to water fields of corn, beans, and squash. Dry farming was perhaps even more important, and the Verde Hohokam built terraces, check dams, bordered gardens, and other devices to capture and divert rainfall and rain runoff onto their fields. One of the more interesting places they practiced dry farming was on the top of tall mesas, which in some places had exceptionally fertile soil and a longer growing season than the valleys below. One such farm exists on Skull Mesa (see the site description that follows), although it has not been shown to have a longer growing season.

The Verde Hohokam also ate a wide range of wild plants including walnuts, acorns, mesquite beans, agave leaves, yucca seeds, and prickly pear seeds. Meat also came from a variety of sources including deer, rabbits, antelope, elk, raccoons, and birds. They also ate fish, turtles, and beaver that lived in the Verde River and its tributaries.

In the way of crafts, the Verde Hohokam differed from most of their contemporaries in that they rarely decorated their pottery. This is not to say, however, that archaeologists have found only plainware at Verde Hohokam ruins. During various periods in their history, these Native Americans traded heavily with the Hohokam of the Salt-Gila basin and other cultures and obtained many decorated pots and bowls from them.

Many Verde Hohokam lived in pithouses or cobblestone pueblos on the lower terraces of the valley. Between A.D. 1125 and 1300, they also introduced cliff dwellings into the area, which they built in the canyons high above the Verde River. The dwellings in Sycamore Canyon, Boynton Canyon, and Towel Creek are a few examples of such ruins and are described elsewhere in this book. More popular examples include the cliff dwellings of Honaki and Palatki near Sedona. The Native Americans' motives for building cliff dwellings are not entirely understood, but some leading theories are presented in the following pages.

In addition to pithouses, pueblos, and cliff dwellings, many "fortified hilltops" in the desert foothills area north of Phoenix have traditionally been assigned to the Southern Sinagua culture, and they will therefore be labeled as Verde Hohokam sites in this book. These include the ruins on Skull Mesa and Elephant Butte just north of the town of Cave Creek, as well as St. Clair Mountain near Horseshoe Lake. As with the fortified hilltops built by the Hohokam proper, the Verde Hohokam hilltops appear defensive. Researchers have also suggested the hilltops served as signaling stations, lookout posts, and living quarters—three more theories that sound similar to the explanations given for the Hohokam hilltops discussed earlier.

After A.D. 1300, the numerous settlements that dotted the Verde Valley consolidated into about fifty large settlements. Some of the better-known villages from this period include the later phases of Tuzigoot, a multistory pueblo near Clarkdale with ninety-seven ground floors, and the later phases of Montezuma Castle, a twenty-room cliff dwelling near Camp Verde. Smaller pueblos and extensive farming areas usually surrounded the large pueblos and cliff dwellings. For example, Montezuma Castle was part of a 200- to 300-person community, making the cliff dwelling itself only a small part of a larger settlement.

The story of the Verde Hohokam ends around A.D. 1425. Nobody knows for sure what happened to them, but they appear to have fallen victim to the same problems that plagued the Hohokam and many other prehistoric southwestern cultures who vanished in the fifteenth century. Drought, floods, disease, warfare, soil depletion, and dissolving trade networks are possible factors that account for their disappearance.

The Verde Hohokam are believed to have descendants among the present-day Hopi Indians of northeast Arizona and probably a few other tribes. Interestingly, many Yavapai claim to be descendants of the Verde Hohokam (or Southern Sinagua), but many archaeologists argue against this, claiming the Yavapai migrated into the area from the Mojave Desert in southern California.

A Verde Hohokam cliff dwelling overlooks Sycamore Canyon.

THE CLIFF DWELLINGS

Some of the best-preserved and most interesting examples of Verde Hohokam architecture can be found in cliff dwellings. The perplexing nature and many questions presented by these sites make visiting these ruins so interesting. Experts are still unclear why Native Americans built their houses so high up on the cliffs and why they chose to live in such rugged canyons instead of on flatter, less treacherous terrain.

As with fortified hilltops, it is almost impossible to look at a cliff dwelling without considering the possibility that it was constructed for defense. The steep slopes and cliffs that surround the fortlike buildings would have provided the Native Americans with an obvious advantage over invaders. The ruins' exceptionally small doorways, many of which stand less than 3 feet high, also may have aided in defense. The tiny entrances would have forced intruders to duck and enter rooms head first, exposing their skulls to whacks by the occupants' clubs.

However, as with the Salt-Gila basin, there is no substantial evidence for conflict in the Verde Valley. This has led to a wide array of less glamorous but perhaps more believable explanations for cliff dwellings. One leading theory, for example, suggests that a period of increased rainfall enhanced the flow of seeps and springs in the canyons. When these previously dry areas began to hold more water, they simply became more attractive places to live.

Cliff dwellings appear to have offered many other weather-related benefits. The massive rocks that support the buildings absorb heat during the day, then radiate it back into the dwellings at night. During winter, this would have made the structures considerably warmer than pueblos built on flat ground. The orientation of the ruins also suggests they were built to battle the cold, for a surprisingly high number of cliff dwellings face south or southeast, enabling them to absorb more sunlight during winter. Conversely, cliff dwellings were great places to escape the summer heat. The buildings are not simply stuck onto the sides of cliffs; they're tucked inside natural rock enclaves. The tops of these enclaves form huge stone overhangs that would have shaded occupants all summer long.

The same rock overhangs that provide shade also would have shielded these Native Americans from rain or any other form of precipitation. This would have been no small benefit during the heavy thunderstorms that characterize Arizona's summer monsoon season.

The waterproof nature of cliff dwellings would have protected the residents' food supply as well. With less moisture to promote the growth of fungi and other microorganisms, corn and other perishable goods could last much longer without rotting. Insects and varmints also would have had more difficulty getting into food stashed in a tightly sealed dwelling on the side of a cliff than in a pueblo on flat ground. Cliff dwellings were so efficient as storage facilities for food that the Native Americans often built small structures called "granaries" solely for that purpose.

Whether built to battle cold, heat, moisture, or all of the above, the insulated quality of cliff dwellings was enhanced by very small doorways. Just as the tiny entrances may have helped keep invaders at bay, they kept out nasty weather and helped maintain internal temperatures.

It seems unlikely that any one of the benefits by itself would have motivated a group of people to live in cliff dwellings. In many ways, life on the side of a cliff would be more uncomfortable than life on the desert floor, so it may have required several benefits combined to make a home among the rocks look attractive. If these people were having difficulty deciding whether their desire to find a more reliable water source justified moving into a cliff dwelling, then a recognition that such a move would also help them store food more efficiently and better fend off enemies may have helped them finalize their decision.

9 Skull Mesa

Type of hike:	Day hike with some bushwhacking, out-and-back.
Total distance:	14 miles.
Difficulty:	Strenuous.
Topo map:	USGS quad—New River Mesa (Trails 247 and 248 not shown on topo map).
Ruin coordinates:	Upper pueblo ("fort") at N33° 56' 56" W111° 55' 54".
Administration:	Tonto National Forest.

To a true hiker, all types of terrain have some sort of appeal. Pine forests have their glamour, rolling prairies possess a more sublime beauty, and rugged desert canyons always hold a certain mystique. However, for all their special qualities, none of these landscapes can provide a hiking experience that beats trekking across the top of a huge mesa that rises high into the air like a big flat island in the sky. If the mesa top also happens to have Native American ruins and petroglyphs, you've got a hiking destination that simply can't be beat—and that's Skull Mesa.

After walking many miles through the desert, climbing more than 2,000 feet, and traversing the top of a humungous grass-covered mesa, you'll finally reach an 800-year-old pueblo built by the Verde Hohokam. The ruin is not located on Skull Mesa proper. It actually sits on a mountain connected to the mesa by a narrow saddle. Half the village sits at the very top of the mountain and half lies just below the summit where the mountain meets the saddle. The upper part of the ruin consists mostly of a rock wall 90 paces long that almost completely surrounds the small flat area at the summit. The wall is several feet thick and reaches a height of about 6 feet at its tallest point. All in all, the upper ruin looks a lot like a fort.

The lower ruin contains about fifteen easily recognizable rooms and, no doubt, many others that are not so conspicuous. The walls are not very tall, but you won't care as much about the walls as you will about what is scattered on the ground. You'll see small pieces of pottery everywhere. A shattered metate lies in the dirt. A small boulder on the edge of the ruin has a deep mortar hole carved into it. You can tell the lower ruin was the center of activity—a true village or hamlet where people lived and worked.

In the very center of Skull Mesa is a field of dark boulders, many of which have prehistoric drawings on them. The pictures include people, lizards, deer, and other animals, as well as various geometric designs and patterns. One of the more notable designs is that of a nicely preserved spiral (see the Hieroglyphic Canyon site description for an interpretation of spirals). Another interesting petroglyph, or set of glyphs, shows two antlered animals standing below a human couple.

The top of Skull Mesa is a beautiful place with spectacular views. However, we still don't know why Native Americans would choose to build a pueblo on top of such a tall, inaccessible mesa. William Holiday, an

Skull Mesa

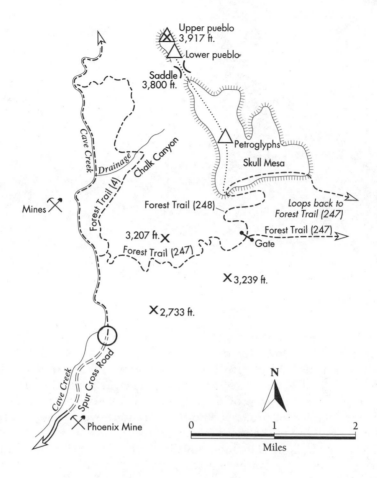

Upper pueblo
3,917 ft.

Lower pueblo

Saddle
3,800 ft.

Cave Creek

Drainage

Chalk Canyon

Forest Trail (4)

Petroglyphs

Skull Mesa

Mines

Forest Trail (248)

Loops back to
Forest Trail (247)

3,207 ft.

Forest Trail (247)

Forest Trail (247)

Gate

3,239 ft.

2,733 ft.

Cave Creek

Spur Cross Road

Phoenix Mine

N

0   1   2
Miles

archaeologist who surveyed dozens of "Southern Sinagua" sites along Cave Creek, considered the possibility that hilltop "forts" in the area were built for defense, but he found it hard to accept the idea because archaeologists have found little direct evidence of conflict in the region. He also noted that while the ruin on Skull Mesa would have provided certain advantages during an attack, the site could have been defended for only a short time before the occupants ran out of water. It would have been as much of a trap as a retreat.

Looking for a better explanation, Holiday noted that the ruin offers sweeping views up and down Cave Creek and that it overlooks a couple of large prehistoric villages at lower elevations closer to the creek. This led him to believe that hilltop sites in the Cave Creek area might have served as lookout posts for the settlements below. Holiday also noted that every hilltop site in the Cave Creek area is visible from another hilltop site, suggesting

This spiral petroglyph is found on Skull Mesa.

that signals might have been sent from one hilltop to the next in order to communicate up and down the drainage very quickly.

The sheer size of the ruin suggests it also functioned as permanent living quarters for at least some Native Americans. The metate and mortar hole, both used to process food, provide additional evidence that the residents stayed in the vicinity for prolonged periods. Holiday even located a prehistoric farm plot on top of the mesa.

Wildlife atop Skull Mesa includes javelina, which hide silently in the tall grass, then flee like pigs out of hell when you step within 20 or 30 feet of them. It's a startling experience—but one that leaves you completely unharmed.

How to get there: The hike up Skull Mesa is a long, uphill affair, and if you want to make it back before nightfall, it's best to head out very early in the morning. If you have an ordinary car, you must drive about 3 miles on a well-graded dirt road, then hike about 7 miles to reach the ruin. The elevation change is approximately 2,100 feet. You'll want long pants for the final 2 miles of the hike, which include bushwhacking through tall grass and a bit of rock climbing.

From the town of Cave Creek, drive north on Spur Cross Road, which splits off Cave Creek Road on the west end of town. After a mile, the pavement on Spur Cross Road ends. About the first 3 miles of the dirt road are well maintained and suitable for any vehicle, but beyond that things get progressively worse. If you have an ordinary car you'll probably want to stop somewhere near the Phoenix Mine, located about 7 miles from the ruin. If you have a high-clearance vehicle, you can push a mile or so farther along the main dirt road.

After parking, hike down the main dirt road paralleling Cave Creek until you reach a sign marking the beginning of Trail 4, which is actually just another old, unmaintained dirt road (if you parked at the Phoenix Mine, Trail 4 will be about 2.25 miles down the road). Turn right onto Trail 4, walk just a bit, then turn right at a sign marking the beginning of Trail 247, which is more of a true hiking trail. Follow Trail 247 for about 2 miles to a barbed-wire fence with a gate. The gate has a rope-and-weight mechanism that causes it to close automatically after you pass through. Immediately after passing through the gate, turn left onto Trail 248. This trail is not marked with a sign, but it's well established, so you can find it easily. Trail 248 will take you about 0.75 mile up a series of switchbacks to the top of Skull Mesa.

When you reach the top of Skull Mesa, leave the trail. It continues along the southern edge of the mesa top and eventually loops back to Trail 247, but it does not lead to the petroglyphs or the ruins. From this point, you must bushwhack north through the tall grass for about 2 miles until you reach the other side of the mesa. You'll find the ruin at the extreme north-west tip of the mesa top. You must go to the absolute farthest point to which you can hike without going down the other side of the mesa. As mentioned, the ruins are not really located on the mesa proper; rather, they're on a cone-shaped mountain connected to the mesa by a very narrow saddle. You'll encounter the lower village first, which lies at the end of the saddle. To reach the upper "fort," continue past the village and climb to the summit. The climb is not long, but it's a bit steep and rocky.

You will pass the petroglyphs on the way to the ruin. They're scattered on a field of dark boulders in the middle of the mesa top, about 0.75 mile from where Trail 248 meets the top of Skull Mesa. If you find one petroglyph, keep looking all around that area because many others will be nearby.

Skull Mesa and nearly all of the hike to reach the ruins are within Tonto National Forest, but the first few miles of Spur Cross Road are not. At this writing, houses were popping up all along the first stretch of the road, and there were big plans to develop a nearby area called the Spur Cross Ranch. This means, among other things, that more of Spur Cross Road may be paved by the time you drive it.

10 Elephant Mountain

Type of hike:	Bushwhack, out-and-back.
Total distance:	About 3 miles.
Difficulty:	Moderate.
Topo map:	USGS quad—New River Mesa.
Ruin coordinates:	N33° 53' 50" W111° 58' 31".
Administration:	Tonto National Forest.

If you want to hike to a ruin along Cave Creek but don't have the time or energy to conquer Skull Mesa, you might want to check out the 800-year-old "fort" on Elephant Mountain.

This place doesn't appear to have any rooms at all, but a huge rock wall at the summit makes the ruin worth seeing. The wall is about 4 feet thick and 80 paces long, and in some of the better-preserved spots it stands more than 6 feet high. It's a classic example of hilltop wall that appears to have been built for defense. Tall cliffs make it impossible to access the ruin from the north, east, or south. The only way a person can reach the top of the butte is to climb up the west slope, which is where the wall stands.

Of course, no good defensive wall would be complete without loopholes, and this wall has plenty of those. Today, a hiker can easily look through the crumbled parts of the wall to get a view of the butte's west slope where access to the summit is easiest. However, when the wall was in better shape, the tiny windows might have provided the only safe way to see who was approaching the mountaintop.

Despite the site's defensive appearance, the archaeologist William Holiday rejected the idea that this ruin might have served as a fort for the same reasons he didn't accept the defense theory for the ruin on Skull Mesa. There isn't much evidence of conflict in the region, and if a hostile group did attack the Native Americans who occupied Elephant Mountain, the invaders could have starved out the defenders in a short time. However, the ruin overlooks a larger prehistoric village closer to Cave Creek, and it's within site of other hilltop ruins, so it may have served as a lookout post or signaling station.

Javelina roam the slopes below the butte in the late afternoon and early morning. You may also see a desert tortoise; I stumbled upon an empty but fully intact shell lying in the shade of a paloverde tree.

How to get there: The hiking part of this trip is only 1.5 miles long (one way, as the crow flies), but it cannot be called easy because there is no trail, the terrain is very rough, and the elevation changes a bit more than 1,000 feet. You'll want long pants for protection against brush and cacti. Before the hike, you must drive 2.5 miles on a well-graded dirt road.

From the town of Cave Creek, drive north on Spur Cross Road, which splits off Cave Creek Road on the west end of town. After about 1 mile, the pavement on Spur Cross Road ends. When you hit the dirt, continue for

Elephant Mountain

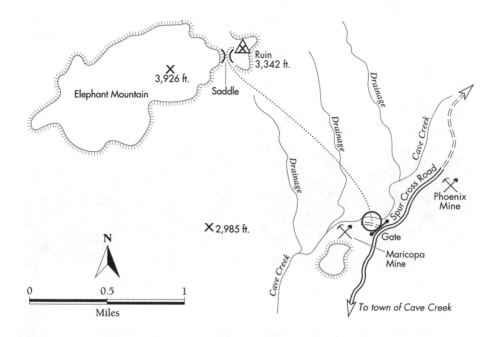

another 2.5 miles to a butte located on the left side of the road. Just past the butte, a smaller dirt road turns off from the main dirt road and heads west for a very short distance to the Maricopa Mine. The road to the mine is blocked by a gate. Park in this area.

Before beginning the hike, it's important to visually locate the butte on which the ruin sits. First find Elephant Mountain, whose peak is located about 1.75 miles to the northwest. It is a tall, elongated mountain that rises about 2,000 feet above the area where you parked (actual elevation is 3,926 feet). The ruin is located on a smaller butte at the base of Elephant Mountain, on the northeast side. A saddle lies between Elephant Mountain and the butte with the ruin. If the big mountain is shaped like an elephant, it could be said that the hill with the ruin forms the head of the animal.

Since no trail leads to the ruin, you need to evaluate the terrain and scope out what you think will be the easiest route. Several drainages come down from the mountain, all of which empty into Cave Creek. The high ground between drainages tends to have less vegetation and makes the best route. Whatever route you choose, remember that cliffs on the north, east, and south sides of the "elephant's head" make access to the ruin from those directions impossible. Make your way to the saddle on the west side of the butte and climb up the hill from there. The big wall is visible from the bottom of the saddle, but you won't be able to see it until you reach that point.

A hiker looks through a crumbled section of the tall stone wall on Elephant Mountain.

As mentioned at the end of the Skull Mesa description, the condition of Spur Cross Road is likely to change—it may become paved—by the time this book is published.

11 Towel Creek

Type of hike:	Day hike, out-and-back.
Total distance:	About 6 miles.
Difficulty:	Moderate.
Topo map:	USGS quad—Horner Mountain.
Ruin coordinates:	Largest ruin at N34° 24' 45" W111° 45' 16".
Administration:	Coconino National Forest.

Here's a destination with three big attractions—some small cliff dwellings, an opportunity to view some interesting wildlife, and a chance to explore a beautiful stretch of the Verde River.

The dwellings were built sometime between A.D. 1125 and 1300 along Towel Creek, a tributary of the Verde located a few miles downstream from the town of Camp Verde. Architecturally speaking, the ruins are simple. The Native Americans found some natural enclaves overlooking the creek and sealed off their entrances with walls of rock and mud.

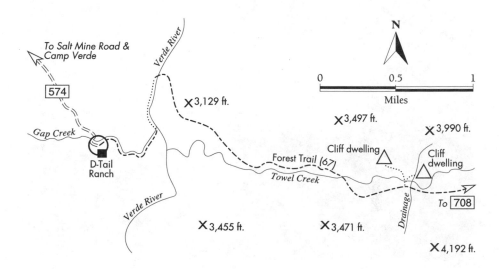

You will find about a dozen enclaves altogether, and you can tell by the sooty "ceilings" that almost all of them were inhabited by humans at one time. Only two of the enclaves, however, still have intact walls. One of the walls is perfectly preserved with a quaint little doorway and a hole near the "roof" that appears to have functioned as a chimney. The other wall has crumbled a bit over the centuries, but it's equally interesting because it still offers protection to the inhabitants who live behind it.

That's right: One of the dwellings is still occupied—not by Native Americans but by bats. At this writing, more than 900 of them lived in the ruin, making it the largest known bat roost in the Verde Valley. They're an eerie but fascinating sight as they cling in tight bunches to the roof of the prehistoric room, wiggling around and squeaking like flying mice. U.S.D.A. Forest Service biologists have not studied the site very much, but they think the animals arc pallid bats and that they only occupy the dwelling during certain months of the year. The bats are definitely home from June through August and possibly even earlier or later than that.

If the bats are not home, you can go inside the ruin, which is filled with huge piles of guano (bat droppings). If the bats are home, *do not go inside!* If you do, you will disturb them. This would create not only an awful ruckus inside the dwelling, but it also could cause the bats to permanently abandon the site. Anyway, it's not necessary to go inside the dwelling because you can get a perfectly good view of the bats by standing outside the entrance and gazing in at them. Do not approach the dwelling in large groups, and be very quiet while you watch the bats. The animals are sensitive to light, so do not shine a flashlight at them or photograph them using a flash.

Note the "chimney" in the upper left corner of the best-preserved cliff dwelling of all the Towel Creek ruins. No bats live inside this particular dwelling.

It's probably worth noting that even though the bats themselves are not dangerous, gasses such as carbon dioxide and methane often accumulate in dank, guano-filled bat roosts like this one, and they can pose a threat to anyone who enters. You also run the risk of getting histoplasmosis, a disease contracted by inhaling fungus spores.

The hike to the cliff dwellings will take you past an exceptionally beautiful stretch of the Verde River. In summer, it's a great place to stop for a swim, especially during the return hike when you're hot and sweaty. If you're an angler, the place is full of giant carp and is said to have a lot of catfish as well. However, unlike the lower Verde River, there are not many bass.

How to get there: This trip requires about 3 miles of driving on a well-graded dirt road and about 8 miles of driving on a poor dirt road that requires some extra ground clearance. The drive is followed by about 3 miles of hiking (one way), mostly on established trails. At one point you will have to wade across the Verde River, which usually contains quite a bit of water. There is also a 200-foot drop over a distance of about 0.5 mile to get down to the river, followed by a 200-foot climb over a distance of about 0.25 mile to get up the other side of the canyon.

From the town of Camp Verde, head west on Salt Mine Road, which begins just north of where Main Street crosses over the Verde River. The road eventually curves south and the pavement gives way to a well-graded dirt road. After driving on the dirt road for about 3 miles, the "main" dirt road turns left toward Beasley Flat and the Verde River. Do not go to Beasley Flat. Instead, keep driving straight ahead on Forest Road 574, which is narrower and rougher. After driving about 8 miles on FR 574, you'll reach Gap Creek, which is marked with a sign. Just after crossing the creek, you reach the D-Tail Ranch. You can drive no farther, so park your vehicle somewhere near the ranch.

Follow the hiking trail down Gap Creek for about 0.5 mile until you reach the Verde River, where the trail ends. The next 0.5 mile follows no trail but is a fairly easy bushwhack anyway. Walk upstream (north) along either bank of the Verde River until you spot an exceptionally large cairn marking a trailhead on the right (east) side of the river. This is Trail 67. It heads southeast, away from the river, toward Towel Creek, then continues up the creek. The trail eventually crosses Towel Creek, but not until you get a lot closer to the ruin.

From the river, follow Trail 67 for about 2 miles. The cliff dwellings will appear high above the creek on the north side of the drainage (on the side opposite the trail). No trails lead up to the cliff dwellings.

12 Sycamore Canyon

Type of hike:	Day hike, out-and-back.
Total distance:	About 14 miles.
Difficulty:	Strenuous.
Topo maps:	USGS quads—Sycamore Basin, Clarkdale.
Ruin coordinates:	N34° 55' 27" W112° 03' 46".
Administration:	Prescott National Forest.

This cliff dwelling overlooking Sycamore Canyon can best be described as a miniature Montezuma Castle without an entry fee, tour guide, or sightseeing crowd. If there was an award for "Best Scenery Surrounding an Indian Ruin," the panoramic view from this site would win it.

Nestled under a natural rock shelter about 0.5 mile from the nearest established trail, the dwelling remains hidden from most hikers who venture into this part of the wilderness. Some people camp for days at a flat clearing just twenty minutes away from the ruin and never even know it's there. However, if you're willing to wander off the beaten path a bit, you're sure to be impressed when you first see the dwelling's ancient walls and mysterious rooms, a couple of which remain almost completely intact.

The site's largest room is tucked into the corner of the rock shelter so that the cliff serves as two of the back walls. The front wall, made of flat slabs of rock held together with mud, stands nearly 20 feet high, and another wall has a tiny doorway hardly more that 2 feet tall.

If you're willing to risk an encounter with a snake, skunk, or some other animal that might live inside the dark room, poke your head through the

Sycamore Canyon

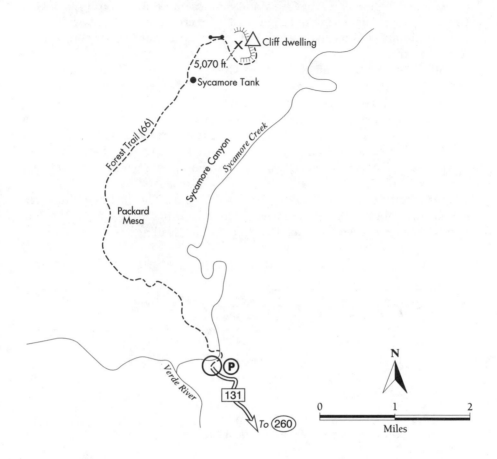

small doorway to see the smoke-blackened wooden ceiling. As an example of prehistoric engineering, the roof is a marvel in itself. A few large beams as thick as telephone poles provide the main support for the ceiling. On top of the large beams lie three more layers of beams, each smaller but more tightly bunched than the layer beneath it. The whole thing is topped off by a watertight seal of mud. With a fire crackling in the corner, the well-insulated room must have provided the occupants with a warm and cozy shelter, even on the coldest and rainiest of nights.

A second room in the opposite corner of the rock shelter remains equally intact, with a small doorway and wooden ceiling much like those in the first room. A handful of broken walls within the ruin and an avalanche of crumbled masonry immediately below the ruin reveal that the dwelling was probably about twice this size when it was built by the Verde Hohokam sometime between A.D. 1125 and 1300.

After exploring the cliff dwelling, take some time to kick back and enjoy one of the best views in Arizona. The lofty vantage point near the rim of

An exceptionally small doorway (note ball cap for size reference) provides entrance into a room still partially covered by a roof made of wooden beams, sticks, and mud.

Sycamore Canyon offers a bird's-eye view of classic red-rock canyons and buttes. All the red is sandwiched between a green juniper forest below and blue sky above, making it a polychromatic sight for sore eyes.

You need a telephoto lens for shooting the ruin's exterior and a wide-angle lens for shooting individual rooms and their interiors.

How to get there: As with most Native American ruins, there are several ways to reach this site. The following route was selected because it offers an opportunity for a scenic day hike. The trip includes a 10-mile drive on a graded dirt road, about 6.25 miles of hiking (one way) on an established trail, and about 0.75 mile (one way) of hiking on a faint, less-maintained trail. The hike begins by dropping about 250 feet in about 0.25 mile, then rising about 1,350 feet over the next mile. After that, however, it's basically flat.

From Cottonwood, take Main Street (Arizona 260) out of town, northwest toward Clarkdale. From AZ 260, turn right onto the unnumbered road leading to Tuzigoot National Monument. (If you get to Clarkdale, you've gone too far; the turnoff is about 0.75 mile southeast of Clarkdale.) Follow the road to Tuzigoot a very short distance to the Verde River, and immediately after crossing the bridge turn left onto Forest Road 131, which is not paved. Follow the dirt road for about 10 miles to a parking area and trailhead at the base of Sycamore Canyon.

Hike down Trail 66 to the bottom of Sycamore Canyon, across Sycamore Creek, and up the opposite side of the canyon. The hike in and out of the canyon is quite a workout, but once out of the gorge the trail veers away from the canyon and onto Packard Mesa, which is basically flat. Continue north across the mesa, then northeast. You will eventually come to Sycamore Tank (watch out for cattle) and, beyond that, a barbed-wire fence with a wooden gate and a sign marking the entrance to Sycamore Canyon Wilderness. At this point, you have hiked about 6.25 miles from the trailhead.

From the gate, the cliff dwelling is about 0.5 mile to the east, as the crow flies (about 0.75-mile hiking distance). To reach the ruin, do not pass through the gate. Instead, turn right down a short stretch of dirt road. At the end of the road begins another hiking trail that heads southeast up to a small mountain pass. The path is rather faint, and it has a few tricky forks, but even if you lose it you can find your way by heading uphill and southeast until you reach the rim of Sycamore Canyon (actually a large tributary of Sycamore Canyon). If you lose the trail on the way up, you should be able to find it again once you reach the canyon rim. Continue on the trail, dropping into the canyon just a bit until you're at the base of a cliff. Then head north for 50 yards or so. The dwelling will appear above you, tucked under a large enclave in the rocks.

13 St. Clair Mountain

Type of hike: Day hike, out-and-back.
Total distance: About 0.5 mile.
Difficulty: Easy.
Topo map: USGS quad—Horseshoe Dam.
Ruin coordinates: N33° 55' 24" W111° 43' 29".
Administration: Tonto National Forest.

Once again the Verde Hohokam built their home in a lofty locale, this time atop a large hill near Horseshoe Lake called St. Clair Mountain. This pueblo features a large spread of foundationlike walls that form as many as twenty easily recognizable rooms, each liberally sprinkled with small pieces of pottery.

The most well-preserved buildings stand at the very top of the hill. There, scraggly rock walls averaging about 3 feet in height form four well-defined rooms. No ceilings remain on any of the rooms, but in prehistoric times the occupants accessed the buildings by climbing through holes in the roofs and down ladders. Entry through the top rather than through the side may have provided better defense against invaders.

Below the summit, most of the buildings have crumbled to mere rock piles, but many walls remain intact enough to show outlines of where rooms used to exist. Emil and Bruce Valehrach, archaeologists who excavated the ruin in the late 1960s, found that the summit and surrounding slopes of St. Clair Mountain had ninety-two rooms when they were occupied sometime

St. Clair Mountain

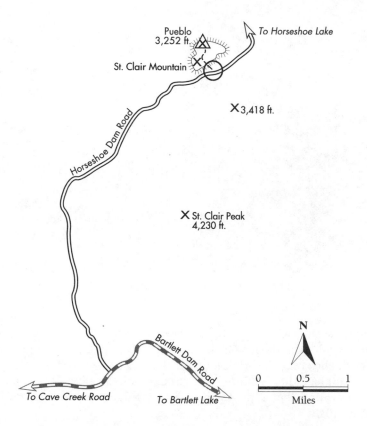

Pueblo
3,252 ft.

To Horseshoe Lake

St. Clair Mountain

Horseshoe Dam Road

X 3,418 ft.

X St. Clair Peak
4,230 ft.

N

Bartlett Dam Road

To Cave Creek Road

To Bartlett Lake

0   0.5   1

Miles

between A.D. 1100 and 1300.

Just as impressive as all the buildings is the abundance of pottery, which litters virtually every spot in and around the site. Most of the sherds are very small, but some are large enough to show the curvature of the pots they once formed.

The 1960s excavation also turned up, among many other things, bracelets made from seashells that had been buried along with many of the pueblo's inhabitants. The arm of one skeleton bore thirteen bracelets, all made from large round shells with their centers bored out almost to the edge so that only a thin rim was left. These bracelets inspired one of the excavators to name the ruin Brazaletes Pueblo, a Spanish reference to the jewelry, and today many people call the village atop St. Clair Mountain by that name.

It is difficult to imagine a person walking 200 miles through the desert to reach the Sea of Cortez, then loading up a basket full of shells and heading back. However, the Hohokam of the Salt-Gila basin did this regularly. Once the shells arrived in the Phoenix area, they probably traded some of them to smaller communities to the north, such as Brazaletes Pueblo.

The best-preserved rooms lie at the summit of St. Clair Mountain.

I encountered a Gila monster at the ruin. With his slithery tongue and pink-and-black skin, the hissing lizard certainly appeared threatening. However, the docile creature didn't look like he could move fast enough to strike a passing ankle. Other wildlife includes deer and javelina, which leave their tracks all around the ruins. In the late afternoon, coyotes yap in the surrounding hills.

How to get there: This trip requires 4.5 miles of driving on a well-graded dirt road. After the drive, you must hike about 0.25 mile (one way) to reach the top of St. Clair Mountain. The 450-foot climb is steep and a bit rocky, but by the time you work up a sweat you'll already be at the ruins.

From the town of Cave Creek, head northeast on Cave Creek Road for about 7 miles until you reach Bartlett Dam Road. Turn right on Bartlett Dam Road and proceed about 7 more miles to Horseshoe Dam Road, which is not paved. Take a left on Horseshoe Dam Road and drive 4.5 miles to a rutty, old, unmaintained dirt road that turns left off the main road and winds its way up a little mountain for about 100 yards. The little mountain is St. Clair Mountain (do not confuse it with St. Clair Peak, which is a little less than 2 miles to the south). The smaller dirt road is not drivable, but it will serve as a portion of the hiking trail, so park where it begins.

Before beginning your hike, note that the top of St. Clair Mountain is actually a ridge with three or four distinguishable "peaks." The ruins lie atop the northernmost peak. You cannot see them from the road.

Begin the hike by walking up the old, small dirt road. When the dirt road ends, a trail begins that will take you right in a more northerly direction toward the ruins. The trail forks many times. There is no best route, as several of the paths branching off from the main trail lead to the pueblo. As long as you keep heading toward the northern peak, you'll reach the ruins.

14 Boynton Canyon

Type of hike: Day hike, out-and-back.
Total distance: About 1.5 miles.
Difficulty: Easy.
Topo map: USGS quad—Wilson Mountain.
Ruin coordinates: N34° 55' 18" W111° 51' 08".
Administration: Coconino National Forest.

If you're up for a short hike and love the red-rock country near Sedona, then take a trip to the Secret Mountain Wilderness, which is part of Coconino National Forest, to see the cliff dwellings of Boynton Canyon.

Once you get past an imposing resort at the base of Boynton Canyon, you'll venture into some truly spectacular scenery. Striking red cliffs rise from the green canyon bottom and meet the blue sky above. Such scenery attracts many hikers to the area, but few visitors climb up the sides of the canyon to see the cliff dwellings; you can expect to find a fair amount of solitude among the ancient buildings.

All of the cliff dwellings in Boynton Canyon were built sometime between A.D. 1125 and 1300. One of the more notable ruins in the area is tucked inside a natural enclave about halfway up the right (east) face of the canyon. The enclave is cut so deep into the rock that you could probably stand inside it during a full-blown thunderstorm and not get wet. The protection offered by the great stone overhang was no doubt an important factor in the decision to build here.

The enclave has also preserved the ruin fairly well, and today you can see two large rooms with walls that still stand up to 5 feet high. One corner of the dwelling even has an original coating of mud that covers the slab-rock masonry like a smooth layer of plaster. A tiny peephole, or loophole, in one of the dwelling's front walls provides a good view of other hikers approaching the ruin, just as it provided the Verde Hohokam with a good view of others approaching their home. A little tree growing from a mossy-green water seep at the back of the rock enclave adds a perfect touch to the dwelling.

Smaller cliff dwellings lie hidden inside other rock enclaves all along both sides of the canyon. In fact, according to a site steward in Sedona who volunteers his time to help protect prehistoric ruins, Boynton Canyon is home to nearly a hundred different archaeological sites. Not all of these, however, are cliff dwellings. You may find faint remnants of other types of ruins and small scatters of potsherds or stone tools.

Boynton Canyon

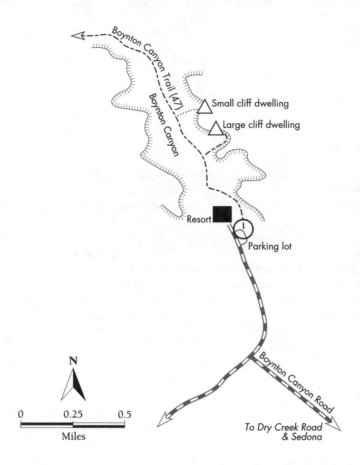

Boynton Canyon Trail (47)

Boynton Canyon

Small cliff dwelling

Large cliff dwelling

Resort

Parking lot

N

0   0.25   0.5

Miles

Boynton Canyon Road

To Dry Creek Road
& Sedona

Whichever ruins you discover, it's a good idea to heed the advice written on a sign near the main cliff dwelling which reads, "Boynton Canyon is sacred to many Indian people. Please show respect and behave as if you were in your church." The sign refers to local Yavapai and Apache Indians whose legends say their ancestors not only built the cliff dwellings in Boynton Canyon but actually emerged from the place in a scenario similar to that of Adam and Eve. The Yavapai-Apache tribes hold annual ceremonies in the canyon that recognize that belief.

Archaeologists believe the Yavapai actually came from the Mojave Desert in California and the Apache came from Canada. However, that doesn't mean their story has no meaning. After all, the story of Adam and Eve is important to Anglos, even if many of the details surrounding the first white man and woman don't quite pan out historically or scientifically.

How to get there: A trip to the main cliff dwelling in Boynton Canyon requires 0.5 mile of hiking (one way) on a well-established trail, followed by

The main cliff dwelling in Boynton Canyon. Note the huge rock overhang.

0.25 mile of hiking on a less-maintained trail that is a bit steep and rocky and rises about 375 feet.

The trailhead is only a few minutes' drive from Sedona. From Sedona, drive south on Arizona 89a, the main strip in town, toward Cottonwood. Before you are out of town, you'll see a street on the right (north) side of the road called Dry Creek Road. Drive north on Dry Creek Road to Boynton Canyon Road. Turn left on Boynton Canyon Road and follow it to a T-shaped intersection. Turn right at the intersection and continue a short distance to a parking space and trailhead on the right side of the road. If you reach the gates of the Enchantment Resort, you have overshot the trailhead just a bit. A guard at the gate will point you in the correct direction if you tell him you want to hike into Boynton Canyon.

From where you park, hike north along Boynton Canyon Trail (Trail 47) for about 0.25 mile until you have gotten around the resort and into the canyon. Once you begin hiking up the bottom of the canyon, continue another 0.25 mile to a smaller path on the right (east) that branches away from the main trail. The smaller trail will take you another 0.25 mile or so up the side of the canyon to the main cliff dwelling.

For overall reference, note that as you hike up Boynton Canyon you pass several smaller canyons feeding into the main canyon. The main cliff dwelling is located inside the second tributary on the right (east) side of the trail. It's under a huge rock enclave about halfway up the north face of the side canyon. The ruin is visible from the Boynton Canyon Trail, although it's difficult to see if you don't know exactly what you're looking for.

The Salado Culture

The Salado culture emerged in the middle Salt River Valley about A.D. 1150. The Tonto basin, which includes the area around present-day Roosevelt Lake, is often thought of as the Salado heartland. Like the people of the Verde Valley, it is believed that these Native Americans developed out of a Hohokam population that had occupied the region for centuries. The gradual transformation into a new culture was caused by prolonged contact, trading, and intermarriage with a variety of non-Hohokam tribes and the adaptations of the Salado to their local environment.

Like their Hohokam ancestors downstream, the Salado used canal irrigation to grow corn, beans, squash, and cotton along the Salt River and its tributaries. The word *Salado* means "salty," a Spanish reference to the waterway near which the group lived. The Salado also harvested many wild foods, including acorns, mesquite beans, paloverde beans, and cactus products. Meat from deer, antelope, rabbits, bighorn sheep, and other wildlife rounded out the Salado diet.

The Salado made many types of decorated pottery, including their hallmark polychrome (multicolored) wares featuring black-and-white designs painted over a red surface. They used their cotton to make beautifully embroidered shirts, skirts, blankets, and other textiles. At the Salado ruins of Tonto National Monument near Roosevelt Dam, visitors today can see the cloth impressions inadvertently made in the walls by Native Americans who were wearing such garments when they leaned against the plaster surfaces when they were still wet. The impressions, which include elbow prints, knee prints, and shoulder prints, imply that the Salado did not simply cover parts of their bodies with cloth; rather, they covered all the major limbs. These Native Americans also made sandals from yucca cordage, jewelry from shells obtained through trade from the Sea of Cortez, and many other impressive items.

Many Salado lived in compounds made of rocks or cobblestones held together with mud. Some also built large multistory pueblos with numerous connected rooms. One of the better known Salado ruins, Besh-Ba-Gowah, in the town of Globe, had more than 200 rooms and housed an estimated 400 people. Other features at some of the major villages included tall walls that encircled the pueblos and large platform mounds like those built by the Hohokam of the Salt-Gila basin.

In addition to their pueblo-style architecture, a small percentage of Salado lived in cliff dwellings. As with the Verde Hohokam, the Salado may have moved into the canyons to be near more reliable sources of water, and their cliff dwellings no doubt provided protection from the cold, heat, and rain. Of course, there is also the defense theory, which, in Saladoland, actually seems to hold a fair amount of weight. Unlike the Verde Valley and Salt-Gila basin, the Salado world contains quite a bit of evidence of prehistoric conflict.

Excavations in the Tonto basin, for example, have turned up stored bundles of human limbs that appear to be trophies of warfare. If you need something a little more convincing, there is always the individual who was found face down in a burned room with an arrow in his back. Competition among different Salado communities over subsistence goods, trade goods, or trade routes may have instigated the conflicts that created these archaeological remains and, ultimately, the construction of cliff dwellings.

Another interesting settlement pattern—one that was for the most part separate from the cliff-dwelling phenomenon—occurred in the mid 1200s. During this time, many Salado moved away from the floodplains along the Salt River and up to rugged hilltops and ridges. The pueblos on Black Mountain and along Tonto Creek site descriptions in later chapters are examples of settlements during this period. The flight of the Salado to higher ground was probably a response to overpopulation in the valley bottom and increased competition for access to the area's irrigated fields. Additionally, a shift in climatic conditions in the mid thirteenth century may have made dry farming in the montane areas look more attractive. Whatever the reasons, the Salado didn't stay in the uplands very long, and most of them returned to the rivers by the year 1280, forced back to their well-watered homeland by a great drought.

Like many other prehistoric cultures in Arizona, the Salado didn't make it to the fifteenth century. The reasons for the group's demise are not entirely understood, although researchers have suggested a variety of possible causes including flooding, internal strife, and warfare.

Like the Hohokam, the Salado probably have descendants among the Pima and Tohono O'odham. A small number of Salado also may have moved to Hopi towns in northeast Arizona.

15 Roger's Canyon

Type of hike:	Day hike, out-and-back.
Total distance:	About 7 miles.
Difficulty:	Moderate.
Topo map:	USGS quad—Iron Mountain (Trail 110 not shown on topo map).
Ruin coordinates:	N33° 27' 51" W111° 12' 30".
Administration:	Tonto National Forest.

If you live in Phoenix and want to hike to a cliff dwelling, the ruin in Roger's Canyon in the Superstition Mountains is probably the closest one you're going to find. It's a pretty good one, too.

You'll encounter the 600-year-old dwelling after a long, dusty drive through classic Superstition scenery and a beautiful hike down the canyon. Most cliff dwellings are built inside rock enclaves, but this place sits inside a true cave. The most prominent structure inside the big cave is a small one-room adobe pueblo that looks more like it belongs in an old Mexican village than in a Salado cliff dwelling. Poke your head through the tiny doorway and you'll see a ceiling made of wood and mud that still covers about three-quarters of the room. In front of the building, a perfectly preserved wall winds its way around a courtyard, acting as a sort of prehistoric picket fence to define the front yard.

The Salado created a second room directly below the big cave by completely covering the entrance to a smaller cave with a wall. It's the only part of the ruin that has a typical cliff-dwelling look. An inviting little doorway in the wall will call you over to peer inside the lower ruin, but you have to be brave to pass through the entrance and into the bowels of such a dark and spooky place.

The two rooms are pretty neat, but what you see today represents only a small part of the original cliff dwelling. The site contained over sixty-five rooms, storage bins, and other chambers when occupied by the Salado. Many of the rooms were situated against the cliff in the lower part of the dwelling, and a ladder on the roof of one of the lower buildings provided access to rooms in the upper cave.

You will not find so much as a potsherd at this site. Previous investigators, however, have found all sorts of items that provide insights into how the Salado lived. Erich F. Schmidt, an archaeologist who excavated the ruin in the late 1920s, found the remains of corn, beans, and squash—the staples of a typical prehistoric southwestern diet. Bones from rabbits, deer, and bighorn sheep revealed that the Salado supplemented their cultivated food with meat from wild animals. Other finds showed that when not hunting or tending their fields, the ancients smoked cornstalk cigarettes and played a game using dice with zigzag geometric patterns on them. Other artifacts included a wooden drill for starting fires, wooden whorls for spinning cotton,

Roger's Canyon

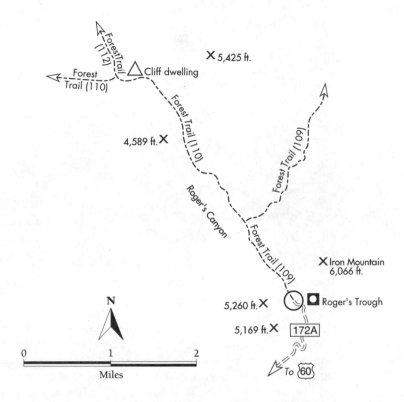

and sandals made from yucca cordage.

Although the Salado culture disappeared by A.D. 1400, the ruin in Roger's Canyon continued to shelter people well into the twentieth century. In the 1920s, a band of outlaws took refuge in the ruin until a posse cornered them inside their prehistoric hideout. In the 1930s, a couple of trappers spent an entire winter inside the dwelling. The two men tore up the place while hunting for pots and other relics, a pastime that significantly reduced the value of the dwelling as an archaeological site. A rock fire circle inside the cave indicates that in more recent times backpackers have spent the night inside the dwelling. The fire ring may plant ideas in your own head, but remember the cliff dwelling in Roger's Canyon is a fragile piece of Arizona's heritage and not a campsite.

How to get there: The 3.5-mile hike (one way) to the cliff dwelling in Roger's Canyon follows a well-established trail. The total elevation change is about 600 feet, which is very mild over that much distance. You'll have to do a bit of rock climbing at the very end to reach the main ruin. Before the hike, there is a 15-mile drive on semigraded dirt roads. A small passenger car could make the trip, but a high-clearance vehicle is highly recommended.

A tiny doorway leads into the "courtyard" of the little pueblo at the Roger's Canyon cliff dwelling.

From Phoenix, drive east on U.S. Highway 60 (Superstition Freeway). About 2 miles past Florence Junction, turn left onto Queen Valley Road. Drive 1.5 miles on Queen Valley Road, then turn right onto unpaved Forest Road 357. Continue on FR 357 for about 3 miles, then turn left onto FR 172. FR 172 eventually becomes FR 172A. Continue on FR 172A to the trailhead and parking lot at Roger's Trough (an old mill).

Follow Trail 109 down the canyon. After a little less than 1 mile, you will come to the junction of Trails 109 and 110. Take Trail 110, which continues straight down the bottom of Roger's Canyon. After a while, the sides of the canyon will become steeper, rockier, and generally more canyonlike. Continue through the dramatic scenery until the canyon veers dramatically to the left (west). After the trail veers left, keep an eye out for the cliff dwelling. It's located on the right, in a cave about 30 yards above the creek.

It would be possible to find the dwelling but only see the small room located in the lower part of the ruin. Make sure you climb above the lower ruin into the two big upper caves to see the main building (shown in photo). The little "adobe house" is located in the least accessible of the two big caves, and access requires a bit of rock climbing.

16 Coon Creek

Type of hike: Day hike, out-and-back.
Total distance: About 8 miles.
Difficulty: Moderate.
Topo map: USGS quad—Dagger Peak.
Ruin coordinates: N33° 43' 39" W110° 51' 19".
Administration: Tonto National Forest.

Heading over to the Sierra Ancha Mountains northeast of Roosevelt Lake, you encounter Coon Creek and a nice little cliff dwelling hidden in the lower part of the drainage. Although fairly small, the ruin is relatively well preserved, and compared to most other cliff dwellings in the Sierra Ancha, it's not very difficult to reach.

This place has all the elements of a typical cliff dwelling. It's located under a natural rock shelter, it overlooks a creek, and it has brownish-red

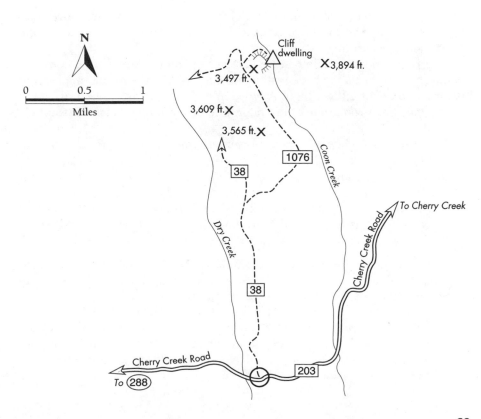

Coon Creek

This room at the Coon Creek cliff dwelling has been nicely preserved.

walls of rock and mud that enable it to blend in perfectly with its surroundings. Of course, if you've never seen a cliff dwelling without a fence around it, this site is as unique as any other.

The ruin's most notable feature is a pair of rooms that share a common wall. The cliff forms the back wall of each room, and the humanmade front walls stand about 12 feet high. A wooden ceiling still covers half of one of the rooms. Each room has a tiny door, one of which has a small peephole next to it.

You'll also find a few other less-preserved rooms around the site, some of which have been reduced to a single standing wall. The entire dwelling had nine ground floors and possibly two second-story rooms when it was built about 700 years ago.

You'll probably notice that the cliff against which the ruin is built has a rich red color. This is due to the presence of an iron-oxide mineral called hematite. In fact, archaeologists refer to this ruin as Hematite House.

How to get there: This trip requires about 7.75 miles of driving on a graded dirt road, followed by about 4 miles (one way) of hiking, mostly on an undrivable dirt road, with no significant elevation change.

From the town of Claypool near Globe, head north on Arizona 88 toward Roosevelt Lake. Turn right on AZ 288 and continue to unpaved Cherry Creek Road (Forest Road 203), which begins about 2 miles past the Salt River. Turn right onto Cherry Creek Road and drive about 7.75 miles until you reach Dry Creek, which is marked with a sign.

Just past Dry Creek, on the left (north), you'll see FR 38, which is marked with a small post. I got stuck twice while negotiating this road in my pickup truck—it is undrivable. However, FR 38 makes a great hiking trail, so stop at this point and put on your boots.

After 1.75 miles, FR 38 forks. Take the road to the right, which is FR 1076. Coon Creek will eventually become visible on the right side of the road. Continue on FR 1076, walking parallel to the creek, to a small mountain pass. Just beyond the pass, a hiking trail appears on the right side of the road. Take the hiking trail a short distance down to the creek. Once at the creek, follow the trail downstream a bit. The ruin will be in a cliff on the right (west) side of the creek.

For an overall perspective on the ruin's location, it's located in the first spot along Coon Creek that begins to box up like a canyon. Downstream from the ruin, the banks come down to the water too gradually to be called cliffs.

17 Black Mountain

Type of hike:	Bushwhack, out-and-back.
Total distance:	About 0.5 mile.
Difficulty:	Easy.
Topo map:	USGS quad—Gisela.
Ruin coordinates:	N34° 05' 56" W111° 19' 47".
Administration:	Tonto National Forest.

The prehistoric pueblo on Black Mountain near the town of Gisela no longer houses Native Americans, but a tribe of century plants has moved into the village and laid down roots right in the middle of many of its tiny rooms. With their tall stalks protruding from between the crumbling rock walls, the agaves appear to be enjoying their hilltop home, which offers sweeping views of surrounding mountains, valleys, and distant Tonto Creek. Other inhabitants in and around the site include tall grass, juniper trees, mule deer, and coyotes. Even without the ruins, it's a scenic destination if you're up for a short but interesting hike.

When you reach the summit of Black Mountain you'll find a large spread of foundationlike rock walls that form a half dozen or so easily recognizable rooms. The original number of rooms was probably much greater than what you can see today. Most of the walls have lost their shape—some sections stand only a few feet high and other areas are crumbled to the ground, but one particularly well-preserved room has intact walls all the way around. Evidently, not much is known about the ruins near Gisela, but the location and style of the pueblo on Black Mountain suggest it was built by Salado

Black Mountain

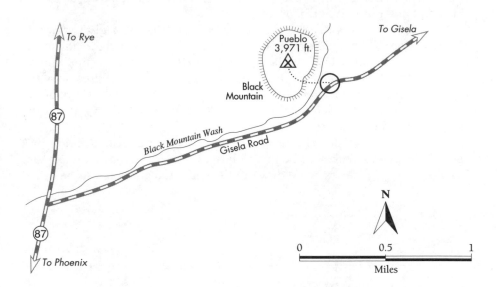

Indians sometime during the thirteenth century.

The hike to this ruin does not take very long. After seeing it, you may want to drive down the road a few miles to the ruin along Tonto Creek, which is described next.

How to get there: This trip includes a 0.25-mile hike (one way) to the top of a mountain that rises about 570 feet from the desert floor. No trail leads to the summit. Wear long pants for protection against the brush.

Black Mountain is an extremely common place name in Arizona. One Black Mountain, located near Tucson, even has Hohokam ruins on top of it.

To reach the site from Phoenix, head north on Arizona 87. Just before the town of Rye, turn right onto Gisela Road. Drive on Gisela Road about 1.5 miles to the base of Black Mountain, which is really a giant hill on the left (north) side of the road. Pull off the pavement and park.

For the most direct route to the ruin, bushwhack straight up Black Mountain to the summit. For a longer but less steep route, make your way around the base of the mountain to the north slope, then climb from there. Either way, you won't see anything until you get to the very top of the mountain.

The Salado built these now-crumbling stone walls at the summit of Black Mountain.

18 Tonto Creek

Type of hike: Bushwhack, out-and-back.
Total distance: About 2.5 miles.
Difficulty: Moderate.
Topo map: USGS quad—Gisela.
Ruin coordinates: N34° 04' 33" W111° 17' 01".
Administration: Tonto National Forest.

If you made the short climb to the ruin on Black Mountain, you may want to explore another Salado ruin just a few miles away on top of a butte overlooking Tonto Creek. This site is roughly the same size as the one near Gisela Road, but it's very different in design.

Unlike the village on Black Mountain, the ruin along Tonto Creek does not have a large number of rooms. Instead, the site's main attraction is a single oval-shaped room about 23 yards long. With an intact wall all the way around that stands 4 feet high in some spots, you may find the great rock structure to be more intriguing by itself than the Black Mountain pueblo in its entirety. At many other archaeological sites in Arizona, large rooms like this have been interpreted as ceremonial chambers.

You'll also find a few smaller rooms around the site and a smattering of walls that don't appear to form any rooms at all. You won't find any pottery, but someone has gathered a collection of prehistoric stone tools and placed

Tonto Creek

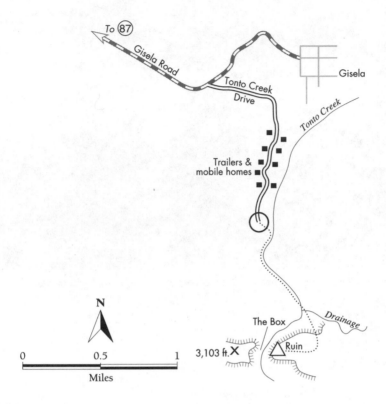

them on top of a flat boulder for display. A trained eye will recognize the crude tools as cutters, chippers, and grinders, but to the layman they look an awful lot like rocks.

For the record, hundreds of other ruins can be found along Tonto Creek. By designating this site as "the" Tonto Creek ruin, I do not intend to imply that it's the only one in the area.

While you're at the ruin, walk through the west doorway of the big oval room and out onto the rocks at the tip of the butte. Then look way, way down into Tonto Creek, and you'll see dozens of monster carp swimming in the pools below.

How to get there: The road to this ruin is paved all the way except for the last mile or so, which is a well-maintained dirt road through a residential area. After the drive, you must hike 1.25 miles (one way) along Tonto Creek. There is no trail, and you will have to cross the creek at least once. The last 0.25 mile of the hike rises about 250 feet. I recommend long pants.

From Phoenix, head north on Arizona 87. Just before the town of Rye, turn right onto Gisela Road. Drive about 4.25 miles on Gisela Road, then, just before reaching the town of Gisela, veer right onto unpaved Tonto Creek

From the outside looking in, the author examines the big room at the Tonto Creek ruin.

Drive. Follow Tonto Creek Drive a mile or so, past all the trailers and mobile homes, to the banks of Tonto Creek. Park somewhere near the creek and put on your hiking boots.

Hike downstream along the creek for 0.75 mile to an area known as the Box. At this point there will be a small "butte" to the left (east), overlooking the creek. For additional reference, a small drainage feeds into Tonto Creek on the north side of the butte. The ruin is on the very top of the butte, so scope out the easiest-looking route and start climbing. You won't be able to see the ruin until you reach the very top.

Sometime during the hike you will have to cross Tonto Creek. At low water levels, you can hop from boulder to boulder without getting your feet wet, but at moderate water levels soaked socks are unavoidable. If the water level looks too high to cross the creek safely, as it often does after a good rain, save the trip for another day.

The Anchan Culture

The Anchans occupied a relatively small region in the Sierra Ancha Mountains of central Arizona. They developed out of an indigenous Archaic population dating at least as far back as A.D. 800, and probably even earlier than that. Around A.D. 1000 they began acquiring many cultural traits that were characteristic of the Mogollon, a people who lived along the Mogollon Rim and other mountainous areas of eastern Arizona and western New Mexico. In fact, some archaeologists lump the Anchans in with the Mogollon.

If there is a heartland of the Anchan world, it is the middle and upper reaches of Cherry Creek, a large drainage leading into the Salt River from the north. It is here that adventurous ruin seekers will find the most interesting Anchan sites, including the subjects of the following three site descriptions.

The Anchans, like the Hohokam, Verde Hohokam, and Salado, grew corn, beans, and squash. However, if you visit any of the ruins located in the rugged, steep-walled canyons leading into Cherry Creek, you will no doubt wonder where the Anchans put their farms. The answer is that they did not actually grow anything in these narrow canyons. They chose instead to farm the relatively flat benches and terraces along Cherry Creek proper, the ridgetops at the mouths of the canyons, and the flats above the canyons. These areas are much too mountainous for canals, so the Anchans used dry farming techniques.

Pottery recovered from Anchan ruins occupied after A.D. 1100 consists mostly of Mogollon types, including a black-on-white variety known as Cibola white, and a black-and-white-on-red ware called White Mountain red. Investigators have also found a significant amount of Salado polychrome, indicating that the people of the Sierra Ancha had quite a bit of contact with the Salado heartland to the southwest.

As far as architecture goes, the Anchans built numerous small, medium, and large stone pueblos along the banks of major drainages and on the tops of high mesas. They also built many fascinating cliff dwellings, especially in the Cherry Creek area. One theory about the cliff dwellings along Cherry Creek maintains that a period of low moisture dried up streams in the lower reaches of the drainage, as well as in lower Coon Creek a little farther west. The canyons leading into the higher parts of Cherry Creek, however, had many seeps and springs that flowed all year long. The perplexing location of the ruins, therefore, may simply represent an effort by the Anchans to find more reliable sources of water.

Not all the Native Americans living in the lower elevations moved upstream when things got hot and dry. In fact, most appear to have stayed in their pueblos. Even those who didn't move up to the cliffs benefitted because when a portion of the population moved away, they left the populations in the larger, lower-elevation settlements with fewer mouths to feed during hard times. Moving some people into the canyons also would have diversified food sources for the overall population. If crops failed in one area, success in another area could compensate for the loss.

The Anchans didn't occupy their cliff dwellings very long. They started building them in the late 1200s and abandoned them in the early 1300s. Such a short residency implies they were responding to a very short-lived condition—so short that at least one archaeologist has suggested that the construction of cliff dwellings could have been a response to a short-term threat by other Native Americans, opening up the possibility that defense, not drought, was the prime architectural influence. Of course, you can also combine the drought theory with the defense theory, because environmental degradation often increases competition for resources. Also, one should not overlook the fact that cliff dwellings provide excellent protection from the elements.

The Anchan culture disappeared by A.D. 1400, probably due to the same list of factors that plagued other prehistoric cultures in Arizona at that time. The Anchans no doubt have descendants among present-day Native Americans, but just who those might be remains a mystery. In fact, much of the Anchan world is a mystery, and the culture remains one of the least known in central Arizona.

19 Pueblo Canyon

<table>
<tr><td align="right">Type of hike:</td><td>Day hike, out-and-back.</td></tr>
<tr><td align="right">Total distance:</td><td>About 6 miles.</td></tr>
<tr><td align="right">Difficulty:</td><td>Strenuous.</td></tr>
<tr><td align="right">Topo maps:</td><td>USGS quads—Aztec Peak, Sombrero Peak (most of hiking trail not shown on topo maps).</td></tr>
<tr><td align="right">Ruin coordinates:</td><td>N33° 50' 37" W110° 52' 59".</td></tr>
<tr><td align="right">Administration:</td><td>Tonto National Forest.</td></tr>
</table>

Bigger isn't always better, but sometimes sheer size has an appeal. The Anchan ruin in Pueblo Canyon is worth its difficult approach on foot simply because it's one of the biggest cliff dwellings described in this book.

When the archaeologist Emil W. Haury ventured into this part of the Sierra Ancha Wilderness in 1930 to gather tree ring samples from the many cliff dwellings in the area, he counted sixty to seventy-five rooms in the Pueblo Canyon ruin. Today, it appears that most of what he saw is still there.

Built like a prehistoric apartment complex, all the rooms lay clustered in three main groups under as many rock enclaves about halfway up the side of the canyon. Many of the dwelling's rock-and-mud walls still stand as tall as the Native Americans who built them, and quite a few rooms reach a second story. One particularly well-preserved building appears to stand three

Pueblo Canyon

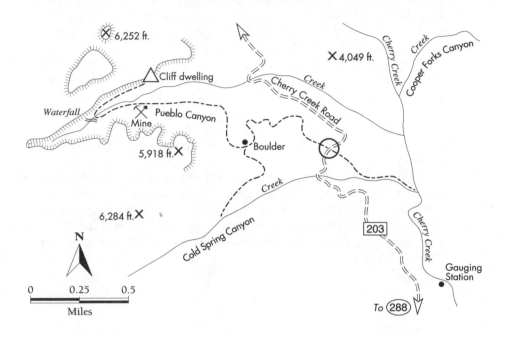

stories high with a partially intact wooden ceiling between the first and second floors.

Many of the rooms have tiny front doorways that look more suited to a hobbit than a human, and the walls between some buildings have small windows for peering from one room into another. Wooden beams the size of telephone poles that once supported roofs or second stories now lie fallen or partially fallen inside many of the buildings.

After being tested, the tree-ring samples collected by Haury revealed the Native Americans cut the earliest wooden beams from nearby trees around A.D. 1290. However, the Anchans didn't live in the dwelling very long; apparently they abandoned the site by A.D. 1330. This makes Pueblo Canyon the last occupied cliff dwelling in the region. The site's relatively late date of occupation and impressive size suggest that a large part of the Anchan population consolidated at the ruin just before abandoning cliff dwellings altogether and returning to flatter terrain.

Why the Anchans chose to live in such a challenging environment is not entirely understood, but as the preceding chapter explains, they may have moved up to the cliffs from lower-elevation settlements to find more water. In fact, if you look around, you can find a water seep or two in the cliffs around the ruin, and you can't miss the waterfall that usually flows at the head of the canyon.

There is one other theory about the Anchans' choice of location that deserves a mention. You won't read about this in any archaeological journal,

Just a few of the multistory prehistoric rooms in Pueblo Canyon that can be seen tucked under natural rock overhangs.

but some people who see the dramatic cliffs, lush ferns, tall pines, and majestic waterfall in Pueblo Canyon believe these Native Americans simply chose to live in the region's most beautiful spot.

How to get there: This trip includes a 23.75-mile drive on a dirt road, the last 4 miles of which require a high-clearance vehicle. After that you must hike about 3 miles (one way) to reach the cliff dwelling. The first mile rises nearly 1,000 feet. Much of the trail is heavily overgrown with brush and can at times be visually difficult to follow. Long pants are recommended.

From the town of Claypool near Globe, head north on Arizona 88 toward Roosevelt Lake. Turn right on Arizona 288 and continue to unpaved Cherry Creek Road (Forest Road 203), which begins about 2 miles past the Salt River. Note your vehicle's odometer reading. The numbers will be helpful later.

After driving 19.5 miles on Cherry Creek Road, you will encounter the Ellison Ranch, located on the banks of Cherry Creek. At this point you must cross Cherry Creek. Once past the creek, the road becomes narrow, rough, and rocky, but passable with a lot of ground clearance.

After about 4.25 more miles (23.75 miles from the paved highway), look for an old, undrivable mining road that approaches Cherry Creek Road from the right, crosses the road, and continues up the hill on the left. For additional reference, the road is located just past a partially buried steel drainage pipe about a foot in diameter that passes underneath Cherry Creek

Road. The old mining road is covered with rocks and overgrown with brush, so keep a sharp eye. Park at the mining road.

From here, begin the approximately 3-mile hike up to the ruins. Walk up the hill (west) on the old mining road until you reach a flat clearing with a good view of Cherry Creek below. On the right (west) side of the clearing you'll find a boulder about 10 feet tall. Turn right at the boulder, onto a less-maintained trail that branches off from the mining road and continues up. The second trail becomes heavily overgrown with manzanita and other shirt-grabbing vegetation and can at times be difficult to follow.

You eventually reach a lookout point on the edge of Pueblo Canyon. Continue up the canyon until the vegetation becomes lush and the trees become tall and shady. From this green patch of forest, look across the canyon to the opposite side to see the main ruins. The dwellings will appear inaccessible, but the trail continues to the top of the canyon, behind a seasonal waterfall, across to the opposite side of the canyon and right up to the ruins. Before reaching the waterfall, you pass a small prehistoric room located near the entrance to a deep, dark mine shaft. The little ruin is interesting, but it's only a small taste of what is yet to come.

A few words of caution about this hike: Ice forms on the trail around the waterfall in very cold weather. The ice can be dark and nearly impossible to see, but if present it could cause you to slip and plummet down the rocky falls. Also, the mine you encounter before reaching the waterfall happens to be a uranium mine, so don't go inside it.

Near the end of your drive up Cherry Creek Road you will pass a Forest Service sign that says there are many cliff dwellings in the area built by a people "currently known as the Salado." The sign is outdated. The "current" boundary line between the Anchan and Salado cultures is now considered to be farther south in the lower reaches of Cherry Creek.

20 Devil's Chasm

Type of hike:	Bushwhack, out-and-back.
Total distance:	About 3 miles.
Difficulty:	Strenuous.
Topo maps:	USGS quads—Aztec Peak, Sombrero Peak.
Ruin coordinates:	N33° 48' 48" W110° 52' 38".
Administration:	Tonto National Forest.

If you hike to enough archaeological sites, you'll come to realize that the splendor of a Native American ruin is usually proportional to the effort required to reach it. That formula certainly applies to the prehistoric buildings in Devil's Chasm. The hike up this treacherous canyon in the Sierra Ancha Wilderness includes very difficult terrain, a lot of poison oak, and an unusually high number of rattlesnakes, but it ends at a spectacular cliff dwelling that makes it all worthwhile.

Actually, if you're the adventurous type, the difficulty of the hike just enhances the appeal of the ruin. As you slash your way through the brush and strain to climb up rocky waterfalls, you can't help but get this feeling like you're searching for some lost Mayan temple or Aztec pyramid. That may sound a bit corny, but such romantic ideas come to life in a very real way when you actually lay eyes upon the cliff dwelling—a nicely preserved 700-year-old ruin that few people ever see.

The ancient structure clings tightly to the side of a cliff high above the creek at the bottom of the chasm. The building's shape conforms to every contour of the narrow ledge on which it sits, and its brownish-red color blends in perfectly with its surroundings. Wooden beams that once supported a roof run through the walls to the ruin's exterior and stick out a foot or so into the air. Placed in a straight row along the entire length of the dwelling, the beams look just like the vigas that characterize today's Mexican haciendas and Spanish colonial homes.

Because of the dwelling's difficult location in the cliff, you cannot simply walk around the perimeter of the ruin to get a closer look. Instead, you must actually enter the building from the side, then make your way through the interior. This is where things really get interesting. You'll duck through one tiny door after another as you move through five different chambers. The walls of every room reach a second story, and one room has walls that tower 20 feet or so above the floor. If you get a bit claustrophobic inside the dim and musty dwelling, peer through one of the small rectangular peepholes in the walls to get a scenic view of the big canyon outside.

In 1930, the archaeologist Emil W. Haury visited the cliff dwelling in Devil's Chasm and concluded that the ruin originally had about fifteen rooms. Tree-ring samples from the wooden beams show construction dates ranging from A.D. 1275 to 1300.

If you are shooting photos, bring wide-angle and telephoto lenses. The

Devil's Chasm

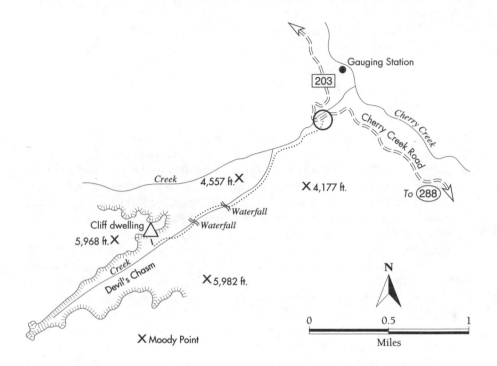

small lens will work well inside the ruin, and the larger one will work well from various vantage points outside the dwelling.

How to get there: As the first part of this site description implies, this ruin is not a destination for those looking for an easy hike. The path leading into Devil's Chasm is very faint and in most places nonexistent, making the trek more of a bushwhack than a trail hike. The brush is dense and contains poison oak plus an unusually high number of snakes, including rattlesnakes. Two points during the hike require some rock climbing. As for distance, the hike is only about 1.5 miles (one way), but with the difficult terrain, 1,950-foot elevation change, and time spent exploring the cliff dwelling, it may take several hours to complete your visit. In addition to the hike, you must drive on a dirt road for 22.25 miles, the last three of which are very rough and require a high-clearance vehicle. Wear long pants for protection against the brush.

From the town of Claypool, head north on Arizona 88 toward Roosevelt Lake. Turn right on AZ 288 and continue to unpaved Cherry Creek Road (Forest Road 203), where you will take a right. FR 203 begins about 2 miles past the Salt River. Note your vehicle's odometer reading. The numbers will be helpful later.

After driving 19.5 miles on FR 203, you will encounter the Ellison Ranch,

When viewed from below, the Devil's Chasm cliff dwelling blends into its surroundings.

located on the banks of Cherry Creek. At this point you must cross Cherry Creek and begin the rough portion of the road. Continue past the Ellison Ranch for about 2.25 miles to another creek. This creek flows out of Devil's Chasm, crosses the road, and goes through an aluminum pipe about 4 feet in diameter on the other side. Your vehicle's odometer should now indicate you've traveled about 22.25 miles on FR 203. You will hike up the creek, so park your vehicle and put on your boots.

A very faint trail begins on the left (south) side of the creek and heads up Devil's Chasm. The farther up the canyon you go, the more faint the trail becomes, until it disappears altogether. You just have to keep trekking up the chasm without it. Navigation is not very difficult, though. Just follow the creek. Keep in mind, however, that the creek forks about 0.25 mile into the hike. Make sure to take the main drainage to the left.

The creek eventually leads into a very narrow gorge, and at the end of the gorge you will find a seasonal "waterfall" (in dry weather, the waterfall may simply appear as a big rock obstacle that plugs up the canyon). You will have to climb up and around the rocky fall. The right side of the fall allows easier climbing than the left.

A second "waterfall," which also is seasonal, lies just beyond the first. If the rocks are dry, the easiest route up this fall will be on the left side. If there is a lot of water flowing in the creek, the left side will be slippery, so climb up the right side.

Continue past the second fall for about 0.25 mile, then look up on the right side of the canyon. Note that there is a huge cliff higher than any other cliff in the area. The ruin is located at the base of the tall cliff, right where the cliff meets the hillside running between the cliff and the creek. You cannot see the dwelling from the creek because it's hidden behind tall trees. In fact, you won't be able to see the ruin until you are within about 50 yards of it.

Getting from the creek up to the ruin is nothing short of an aerobic workout. Fortunately, the trail miraculously reappears at this point, and it will take you right up the hill to the dwelling. When you reach the dwelling, remember that it is accessible only from the left side.

The 700-year-old walls of this ruin are fascinating because they are exceptionally tall. However, this also makes them more prone to falling down, so take extra care not to lean or climb on them.

21   Cooper Forks Canyon

Type of hike:	Bushwhack, out-and-back.
Total distance:	About 3 miles.
Difficulty:	Strenuous.
Topo map:	USGS quad—Sombrero Peak.
Ruin coordinates:	N33° 50' 02" W110° 51' 34".
Administration:	Tonto National Forest.

Perched high at the rim of Cooper Forks Canyon, a rugged gorge in the Sierra Ancha Mountains, this cliff dwelling is one of the more intimidating archaeological sites described in this book. You can actually see it from the dirt road leading to the ruin, but when you spot the tiny brown buildings far up near the canyon's rim, you'll gasp at the prospect of climbing up to reach them. However, on a cool day the hike is actually rather nice, albeit steep.

According to a 1930 archaeological survey of the Sierra Ancha, the dwelling originally had twelve rooms when it was built around A.D. 1304. Today, you'll see only half that many rooms, but those that do remain make the trip well worth the effort. One of the buildings still stands two stories tall, and another has a perfectly intact roof complete with wooden beams, sticks, and mud. Another room, located higher than the others inside a little cave, connects with a second room in a lower cave via a small tunnel within the rocks. It's a peculiar layout, for any type of dwelling.

You'll find a bit of pottery at this site. You can also see the shattered remains of a couple of metates and manos.

How to get there: As mentioned, a trip to the ruin in Cooper Forks includes a long, steep climb up the side of the canyon. The climb rises roughly 1,200 feet over a distance of about 0.75 mile. Most of the route follows no recognizable trail. In addition to the climb, the trip includes a 0.5-mile boul-

Cooper Forks Canyon

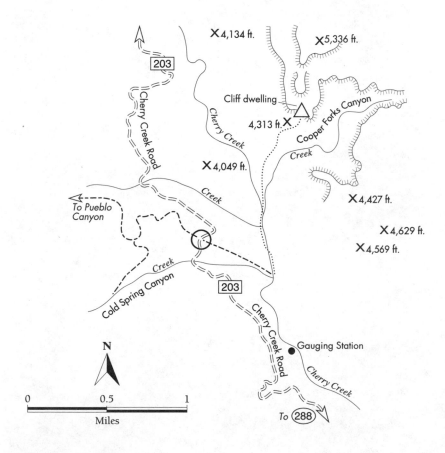

der hop along Cherry Creek and a little jaunt down an old dirt road that bring the total hiking distance to about 1.75 miles (one way). Before the hike, you must drive on a dirt road for 23.75 miles, the last 4 miles of which require a high-clearance vehicle. A pair of binoculars will help a great deal in locating the cliff dwelling.

From the town of Claypool, head north on Arizona 88 toward Roosevelt Lake. Turn right on AZ 288 and continue to unpaved Cherry Creek Road (Forest Road 203), which begins about 2 miles past the Salt River. Take a right on FR 203. Note your vehicle's odometer reading. The numbers will be helpful later.

After driving 23.75 miles on FR 203, look for an old, undrivable mining road that approaches FR 203 from the right, crosses the road, and continues up the hill on the left. For additional reference, the road is located just past a partially buried steel drainage pipe about a foot in diameter that passes underneath FR 203. The old mining road is covered with rocks and overgrown with brush, so keep a sharp eye. Park at the mining road.

Built inside a large rock enclave, these rooms in the Cooper Forks cliff dwelling still stand two stories high.

At this point, it is very important to visually locate the cliff dwelling in order to get an idea of where you are going. Walk up FR 203 a block's length or so to a lookout called Pottery Point with good views across Cherry Creek and into Cooper Forks Canyon. From there, you can see the tiny ruin on the left (north) side of the canyon. It's way up near the rim where the canyon's slope meets the base of a sheer cliff. You may need binoculars to see it if you do not have good vision.

After locating the ruin, go back to where you parked and walk down the hill (east) on the old mining road for about 0.5 mile until you reach Cherry Creek, which usually has a lot of water. There are no useful trails beyond this point.

Hike up Cherry Creek, either along the banks or by hopping from one boulder to the next. After hiking upstream for about 0.5 mile, you'll reach the mouth of Cooper Forks Canyon on the right.

Near the mouth of Cooper Forks Canyon are a couple of trails that will take you up the north side of the canyon toward the ruin. Unfortunately, they both fizzle out after a few hundred yards. All you can do from that point is bushwhack up the canyonside until you reach the ruin.

The Perry Mesa Tradition

We often assume that all Hohokam villages share more or less the same qualities or that the Native Americans who occupied one Salado settlement were nearly identical to those in another. In actuality, Arizona contains countless archaeological sites that share traits with two or more neighboring cultures, creating a taxonomic challenge for the researchers who study them. Conversely, such ruins may also have characteristics not found in any nearby settlement, making it difficult to lump them in with any of their neighbors. The people of Perry Mesa were a prime example of Native Americans who fell into one of prehistory's cultural gray areas.

Perry Mesa is not really a mesa, at least not in the common sense of the word. It's more like a gently rolling prairie that stretches from Bloody Basin Road near Cordes Junction south almost to Black Canyon City and from Interstate 17 east about 10 miles to Hutch Mesa. The 75 square miles of grassland also features an occasional stand of juniper or prickly pear, and the area is traversed by several rugged canyons that drain into the upper Agua Fria River. This contrasting mix of flatlands and deep gorges is often referred to as a "mesa-canyon complex."

In addition to being a place of great natural beauty, Perry Mesa is home to an exceptionally high concentration of Native American ruins occupied primarily during the fourteenth century. The largest ruins are clustered into "seven cities" of stone spread throughout the region. Each pueblo contains a hundred or more rooms, and some originally had two or more stories. Most of the large settlements also have smaller satellite pueblos surrounding them. All the villages were built near the rims of canyons for easy access to the water flowing in the streams below, and it was very common for the occupants to decorate the rocks along the rims with impressive displays of petroglyphs.

The architecture of the Perry Mesans shares many traits with that of neighbors in all directions, especially the Salado. However, there are striking differences as well. The people of Perry Mesa never bothered with ball courts, platform mounds, or any other large forms of public architecture. Even internal plazas and community rooms are noticeably absent from most of their big stone villages. One of the few structures that might have served a communal purpose is a mysterious and little understood structure informally called a "racetrack." Measuring about 5 meters wide and up to 200 meters long, racetracks look like rock-lined roads that lead absolutely nowhere. This unique "public architecture," or lack thereof, may reflect unique religious beliefs or a social structure different from that of neighboring cultures. All the sites described in the following pages contain racetracks that have not withstood the test of time very well, so it's unlikely you'll be able to find them.

As with the Hohokam, the Verde Hohokam, the Salado, and the Anchans, the people of Perry Mesa were farmers who grew corn and other crops.

Since canals don't work very well on top of a mesa, the Native Americans relied on rainfall to water their fields. That is not to say that their agricultural techniques were unsophisticated, for they enhanced the productivity of their dry farms by lining them with complex stone devices that routed rain runoff toward their crops, and they dug huge terraces to conserve the soil.

Great herds of antelope once grazed the lush grasslands on Perry Mesa, and the human population no doubt hunted the wild game. Additionally, archaeological excavations have uncovered charred deer bones, blackened rabbit bones, and, somewhat surprisingly, a rather large number of cooked coyote bones.

Like the Verde Hohokam, the Native Americans on Perry Mesa rarely decorated their pottery. They didn't really have to, since they obtained polychrome wares from the Salado and other colorful styles from the Hohokam. They also used quite a bit of Jeddito ware, a striking black-on-yellow style imported from a Hopi town in the Verde Valley. In addition to regular jars, pitchers, and bowls, the Perry Mesans made human-shaped vessels, bird-shaped effigies, toad-shaped vessels, and other impressive ceramic works.

Rings, bracelets, and necklaces made of seashells have also been recovered from the pueblos on Perry Mesa. One prehistoric infant was found buried with a shell pendant overlaid with turquoise and other colorful stones. Other noteworthy craft items include whistles and smoking pipes made from animal bones.

It's hard to apply a specific cultural classification to the people of Perry Mesa, and even experts have had a hard time defining them. This is partly because the Perry Mesans share many qualities with all of their neighbors and partly because they have many unique traits. Also, there has been more vandalism and pothunting on Perry Mesa than scientific research. Hence, we are left with a culture that we may never come to understand. Today, the people of Perry Mesa are simply considered to be part of the "Perry Mesa tradition."

22 Perry Tank Canyon

Type of hike:	Day hike with some bushwhacking, out-and-back.
Total distance:	About 10 miles.
Difficulty:	Strenuous.
Topo maps:	USGS quads—Joe's Hill, Brooklyn Peak (beginning of Road 481 not shown on topo map).
Ruin coordinates:	N34° 12' 00" W112° 04' 16".
Administration:	Bureau of Land Management.

The pueblo at the rim of Perry Tank Canyon contains about 150 rooms. That alone makes the site worth seeing, but perhaps even more impressive than the ruin's size is the elaborate display of rock art nearby.

One of the more noteworthy petroglyphs near the pueblo is shaped like a duck. In fact, the image is so peculiar that the entire ruin is officially called *Pueblo Pato*, which translates very loosely to "Quack House" from Spanish. The duck is pecked onto the side of a cliff just below the ruin along with two deer and a human. The four creatures, all standing in a row, have a cartoonlike appearance that can only be described as comical.

Other petroglyphs near the ruin are equally striking, not so much for their shape as for their size. You'll find pictures of deer as big as small dogs, and a few human-shaped glyphs at the site are as large as preschool-age children.

As for the pueblo, the walls no longer stand very tall, but you can easily make out rooms among the rubble. The rooms are spread over a fairly wide area, but you'll find one exceptionally large compound containing sixty-five to seventy rooms packed as tightly as holes in a beehive. The whole area is covered with small pieces of plain-colored pottery, and if you look very hard you may find the remains of a metate and mano or two.

Keep an eye out for antelope as you hike to this ruin. The animals run swiftly over the mesa and all change direction at once, just like a flock of birds. They make a spectacular sight, one that must have been very common for the Native Americans who lived in Pueblo Pato.

How to get there: The following suggested route to Pueblo Pato requires about 11 miles of driving on a graded road, 1.25 miles of driving on a poor road, and 5 miles of hiking (one way). There is no elevation change worth worrying about, but you must do a bit of rock climbing in order to see all the petroglyphs. You'll need a high-clearance vehicle for the last mile of driving and long pants for protection against the tall, itchy grass. A compass may come in handy.

If you begin the trip in Phoenix, head north on Interstate 17 and turn right on Bloody Basin Road (Forest Road 269), an unpaved but well-graded road located about 3 miles south of Cordes Junction. Drive on FR 269 for about 11 miles, then turn right onto FR 14.

FR 14 is narrower than FR 269 and fairly rough. Drive south on FR 14 for

Perry Tank Canyon

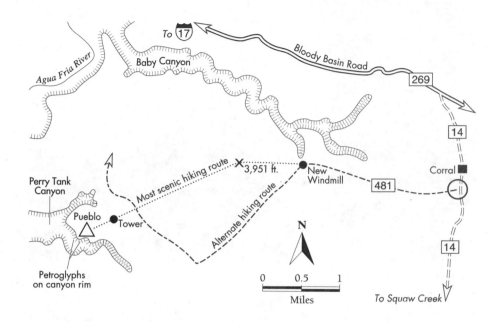

about 1.25 miles to the intersection of FR 14 and FR 481. FR 481 is the first crossroad you will encounter *after* passing through a corral with two cattle gates. (USGS topo maps do not show this section of FR 481. They do, however, show a crossroad you will encounter *before* passing through the corral, which you should not take.) This is not private land.

Things start to get really rough here. In fact, beyond this point the road is so narrow and rutty that you'll probably be better off using it as a hiking trail, so park and put on your boots. Hike west along FR 481 for about 2 miles to a windmill, called the New Windmill.

At this point you have two choices. If you continue on the road, it will take you southwest for about 2 miles, then northwest for about 1 mile, at which point you will be pretty close to the ruin. However, it is highly recommended that you bushwhack from the New Windmill straight ahead (due west) to the top of a big, gently sloping hill about 200 feet tall. The climb is easy, and it's about a mile long. Once you reach the top of the hill, you will have outstanding views of Perry Mesa in all directions, plus a very good chance of spotting a herd of antelope somewhere out on the grass-covered "plains."

From the scenic hilltop, the ruin is located a little more than 2 miles away at 241°, on the rim of Perry Tank Canyon. A compass comes in handy at this point. One particularly convenient landmark is a large metal APS transmission line tower (telephone pole) that is very close to the archaeological site

The duck petroglyph at Perry Tank Canyon can be seen near two deer figures and a human one.

and also at 241° from the hilltop. Be careful not to confuse it with several other towers in the distance.

Once you reach the tower, continue southwest about 0.25 mile or so to the north rim of Perry Tank Canyon. You shouldn't have any problem finding the ruin, but finding the petroglyphs is a bit tricky. Half the glyphs are located just west of the ruin, on the rocks just below the rim of Perry Tank Canyon. You must actually climb down into the canyon a bit to see them. The rest of the glyphs, including the duck, are located on the southwest side of the ruin, and again, you must climb down into the canyon a bit to see them. The duck is located farther down the canyon than most of the other petroglyphs; you won't see it until you're standing right in front of it.

23 Squaw Creek

Type of hike: Day hike, out-and-back.
Total distance: About 5 miles.
Difficulty: Moderate.
Topo maps: USGS quads—Joe's Hill, Brooklyn Peak.
Ruin coordinates: N34° 07' 52" W112° 00' 24".
Administration: Tonto National Forest.

As with the Perry Tank Canyon pueblo, the most interesting thing about the Squaw Creek ruin is not its crumbling old buildings but its fantastic display of petroglyphs. Like the other ruin, this place has a few odd ones.

There are no ducks at this site, but you'll find a lot of deer. What makes the animals so unusual is that a few of them are painted red. The paint is unusually well preserved, making the deer stand out well among the nonpainted petroglyphs surrounding them. The practice of painting petroglyphs was actually not that uncommon in prehistoric times. Many

Squaw Creek

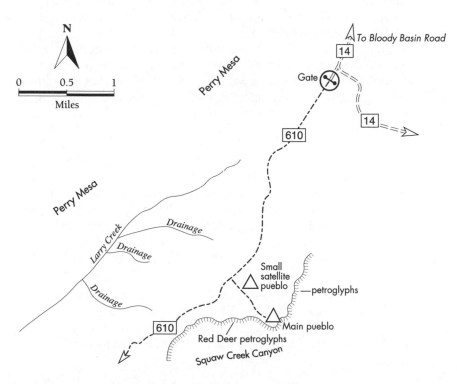

This deer petroglyph at the Squaw Creek ruin is painted red.

petroglyphs in Waterfall Canyon in the White Tank Mountains, for example, were colored by the Hohokam. We just don't see colored glyphs very often because the paint usually weathers away over the years, leaving images that today look like ordinary petroglyphs.

The vast majority of glyphs at the Squaw Creek ruin are not painted, but they're still interesting. Plain-colored deer and bighorn sheep are all over the place, and odd-looking people show up here and there. Other images include grids, peculiar dot patterns, bull's-eyes, spirals, and something that resembles a big steering wheel with a spiral in the center.

With about 150 stone rooms, the Squaw Creek ruin is one of the largest prehistoric pueblos within Tonto National Forest. Most of the rooms are surrounded by a fairly well-preserved wall that appears to protect the site on all sides, except for one side that borders a natural cliff. It takes more than three minutes to walk the entire length of the wall—about the same amount of time it takes to walk a city block. There is also quite a bit of pottery scattered around the site, especially inside the walled area.

Most people seem to call this site the "Squaw Creek ruin," but it is sometimes referred to as *Las Mujeres,* which translates from Spanish as "The Women."

How to get there: This trip includes about 18 miles of dirt roads (one way). About the first 11 miles are well graded, the next 4.5 require high-clearance vehicles, and the remaining 2.5 are more suited to hiking than driving. The hike is flat. However, once you reach the ruin, you'll have to do a bit of rock climbing to see the petroglyphs. You'll want long pants for protection against all the brush around the glyphs.

If beginning the trip from Phoenix, head north on Interstate 17 and turn right (east) on Bloody Basin Road (Forest Road 269), an unpaved but well-graded road located about 3 miles south of Cordes Junction. Drive on FR 269 for about 11 miles, then turn right onto FR 14.

FR 14 is narrower than FR 269, and it is fairly rough, especially in areas where it crosses creeks. Drive south on FR 14 for 4.5 miles to FR 610, which veers off to the right a bit. There is a cattle gate at the beginning of FR 610. There is also a post with the number 610 on it, although at this writing the white numerals were peeling off the dark-brown post.

FR 610 is even worse than FR 14, so you may not want to continue driving. If not, park and walk down the road for about 2 miles until you reach yet another road that turns left (south). This unnamed road is the worst yet, but it's great for hiking and it's only about 0.5 mile long. Follow the road southeast (the only way you can go) to the north rim of Squaw Creek Canyon and all the ruins.

You shouldn't have any problem finding the ruin, but the petroglyphs are a bit tricky to find. Most of them are located just east, and just south, of the ruin. They're just below the rim of Squaw Creek Canyon, and you must actually climb down into the canyon a bit to see all the good ones, including the red deer.

24 Silver Creek

Type of hike:	Day hike with optional bushwhacking, out-and-back.
Total distance:	About 3 miles (to main ruin and back).
Difficulty:	Easy.
Topo maps:	USGS quads—Cordes Junction, Joe's Hill.
Ruin coordinates:	Main ruin at N34° 15' 07" W112° 01' 47", "Fort" at N34° 15' 09" W112° 02' 35".
Administration:	Bureau of Land Management.

Silver Creek supports the theory that the splendor of a Native American ruin is equal to the effort required to reach it. This place is much easier to get to than Squaw Creek or Perry Tank Canyon, but you won't find any rock art when you get there.

The site, however, is still worth seeing. Called *Pueblo La Plata* because of its location on the south rim of Silver Creek, it probably has more rooms than the average person is willing to count. According to scientific literature, the pueblo originally had 120 to 160 rooms.

Most of the walls are crumbling all over the place, but if you look near

Silver Creek

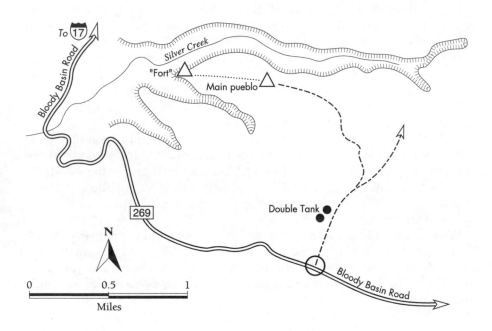

the foundations you can see neatly worked masonry, revealing that once all the walls were nice and smooth with perfectly square corners. As with most ruins on Perry Mesa, the rooms also seem to be quite a bit larger on average than those found in Hohokam pueblos farther south.

The whole ruin is located on a big mound about 6 feet high. It looks as if the inhabitants simply wanted a good view of the surrounding terrain, since the little hill could not have afforded much protection from an invasion. If you want to see true defensive architecture, you'll have to hike about 0.5 mile due west of the ruin to the very tip of the mesa. There, you'll run into a great wall 70 paces long and up to 8 feet high that forms what looks like a fort. There are many such "forts" on Perry Mesa. They are believed to have been built as guard villages during the thirteenth century, before the Perry Mesans congregated into their seven large "cities." It has even been proposed that outside groups who wanted to move onto Perry Mesa during the thirteenth century had to earn their admission by manning the forts and providing military service. Once the people of Perry Mesa began congregating into their large pueblos in the fourteenth century, the size of their settlements alone was probably sufficient to deter enemies and the forts were no longer needed.

There is quite a bit of pottery among the ruins, especially around the main pueblo.

The author stands just outside the entrance to a crumbling old room at the Silver Creek ruin.

How to get there: The trip to Pueblo La Plata includes 8.75 miles of driving on a well-graded dirt road, followed by 1.5 miles (one way) of easy hiking. The hike is flat. No special clothing is needed, unless you want to bush-whack an extra 0.5 mile to see the "fort," in which case you'll need long pants.

From Phoenix, head north on Interstate 17 and turn right on Bloody Basin Road (Forest Road 269), located about 3 miles south of Cordes Junction. FR 269 is unpaved but well maintained. Drive on FR 269 for 8.75 miles to a smaller, unnumbered, poorly maintained road that turns left (north) toward a couple of large watering holes for cattle, which together are called the Double Tank.

Park at the base of the road and walk about 0.25 mile north to the tanks. *Immediately* after passing the water, look for an even less-maintained road that veers off to the left, then heads west. The road is faint, but it is critical that you find it. If you continue walking on the better road you will head northeast and never find the ruin. After making the turnoff at the Double Tank, walk another 1.25 miles or so and you'll bump right into Pueblo La Plata.

If you want to see the fort, bushwhack due west from the ruin for a little more than 0.5 mile. There is no way you can miss it because the canyons to the north and south will funnel you to the tip of the mesa where the fort is located.

The Ancestral Pueblo (Anasazi) Culture

The Ancestral Pueblo people occupied a large chunk of the Southwest that included northern New Mexico, northern Arizona, southern Colorado, southern Utah, and a bit of southern Nevada. The Four Corners area is generally considered the cultural epicenter of this vast region.

Since the Ancestral Pueblo world is so big, archaeologists divide it up into subregions, each of which contains relatively similar pottery styles and architectural forms. These subregions include Virgin (Virgin River area in southwest Utah and northwest Arizona); Kayenta (primarily northeastern Arizona and the Grand Canyon); Little Colorado (primarily the north-central part of east Arizona); Mesa Verde (the Four Corners area, especially southwestern Colorado and southeastern Utah); and Chaco (Chaco Canyon area in northwestern New Mexico).

The name "Ancestral Pueblo" is a reference to the fact that these people are ancestors of modern Native Americans who still live in pueblos. The Ancestral Pueblo people have traditionally been called the Anasazi, which is a Navajo word meaning "ancient enemies" or "enemy ancestors." The word Anasazi is considered derogatory by some people and is therefore being replaced by the updated name.

Since Ancestral Pueblo people lived farther north than the Hohokam, Salado, and most other "high cultures" of the Southwest, it took a bit longer for Mesoamerican innovations such as agriculture and pottery to reach them. The Mexican influence arrived, nevertheless, and by A.D. 500 corn, beans, squash, ceramics, and other new technologies had transformed Archaic Indians throughout the region into a new culture, the Ancestral Pueblo.

The first Ancestral Pueblo people lived in pithouses sunk several feet into the ground. The pithouse roofs consisted of large wooden beams that supported a finer composition of sticks and mud. Around A.D. 700, the Ancestral Pueblo people began making above-ground homes called jacal, which consisted of mud and interwoven branches placed over a framework of wooden poles. Pithouses, however, were still used for communal purposes and as dwellings when it was very cold.

Early Ancestral Pueblo settlements were relatively small and often situated around a kiva. These structures, which were built at least partially underground, evolved around A.D. 750 from the old pithouses. Access to kivas was usually by ladder through a hole in a roof. Inside was a firepit and a small sacred hole called a *sipapu*, which symbolized the Native Americans' belief that their ancestors came from within the earth. The interior walls were often decorated with paintings of deities, corn, rain clouds, and other items of great importance.

The Ancestral Pueblo community probably used kivas in much the same way modern Pueblo people do. If so, the subterranean rooms served as communal structures, places for prayer and religious ceremonies, and as schoolhouses where young men were taught everything adults needed to know. Kivas also functioned as workshops, especially in bad weather. The warm and highly protective structures would have made ideal places to make weapons, spin cotton, or weave cloth. In modern Pueblo cultures, males spend a great deal of time in kivas. Females, on the other hand, are not allowed to enter unless they must watch or participate in an important ceremony. This may have been the case in prehistoric times as well, but nobody knows for sure. Several ruins described in the following pages, including the sites in Grand Gulch and Cottonwood Canyon, have kivas.

The kivas just described were only large enough to accommodate a single family. A bit later in their history, the Ancestral Pueblo people made "great kivas" that could accommodate multiple families. Great kivas had some different structural features, and rather than being built in every village, they were placed in centralized locations to serve as meeting places for numerous communities.

Around A.D. 900 these Native Americans began constructing small, single-story masonry pueblos. The stone homes were usually located on flat, open ground and were surrounded by farms. Over the centuries, single-story pueblos evolved into multistory pueblos with hundreds of rooms and smooth, refined masonry that rivals modern brick buildings. Along with the increase in building size came an increase in the overall size of settlements. By the twelfth century, most small villages had aggregated into large communities, some with a thousand or more residents.

Around A.D. 1100 another striking form of architecture emerged—the cliff dwelling. The Ancestral Pueblo people developed this form of architecture perhaps more than any other Native Americans. However, only a small percentage of the population actually lived among the rocks. Even after A.D. 1100, most occupants lived in pueblos.

The remarkable appearance of Ancestral Pueblo cliff dwellings has created a perception among many people that these Native Americans were the most advanced culture in the prehistoric Southwest. They were indeed advanced, but it is important to remember that cliff dwellings resist erosion better than other types of ruins because they are built inside natural rock enclaves. Cliff dwellings have also remained relatively unharmed by present-day activity because they're often located in canyons that are too rugged to develop. If the large, multistoried pueblos built by many other Indians of the Southwest had not been obliterated by centuries of wind, rain, and European settlement, people today would be able to see easily that several other prehistoric groups were just as sophisticated. The elaborate system of Hohokam canals, if it was still intact, also would make a strong impression on the general public.

As mentioned, the Ancestral Pueblo people grew corn, beans, and squash. Crops of lesser value such as sunflower and cotton were also grown. They did not make extensive use of canals, but they built many dams, terraced arroyos, reservoirs, and other mechanisms to capture rainfall and control soil erosion. They also domesticated turkeys, which they used for feathers as well as food. In addition, Ancestral Pueblo men used nets, snares, and bows and arrows to capture and kill deer, antelope, elk, bighorn sheep, rabbits, squirrels, raccoons, wood rats, grouse, and other wild game. Women cooked and gathered acorns, walnuts, pinyon nuts, prickly pear cactus, and a variety of wild seeds and fruits.

The Ancestral Pueblo people made petroglyphs and pictographs that, in my opinion, are more impressive than the rock art of other cultures described in this book. A typical Hohokam image of a man, for example, looks much like a simple stick figure, while Ancestral Pueblo humans are often depicted as horned dancers, shield figures, or broad-shouldered characters with triangular bodies. The Ancestral Pueblo people also drew Kokopelli, the humpbacked flute player who now decorates modern T-shirts, lamps, lawn ornaments, coasters, paperweights, and a million other kitschy products. Kokopelli has become such a popular design with today's merchandisers that his name and image pops up regularly in places around the United States where the ancient musician is not even an indigenous character. Other common Ancestral Pueblo rock art motifs include human handprints, which are usually painted red or white.

Picasso once said, "Good artists borrow. Great artists steal." The Ancestral Pueblo Indians were aware of this concept. Research in Utah's Canyonlands National Park suggests many rock art images found in the northern Ancestral Pueblo region—including shield figures, ghost figures, and horned dancers—were borrowed from the Fremont culture, whose heartland was along the Fremont River and covered most of Utah. The Fremont lived at about the same time as the Ancestral Pueblo people. Although not covered in this book, Fremont rock art sites are very impressive, and if you ever visit Nine Mile Canyon or similar places in Utah you will easily understand why another culture would be prompted to copy Fremont artwork.

The hallmark of Ancestral Pueblo pottery is the simple but elegant black-on-white style. Small sherds bearing these colors can still be found easily at many ruins, including those in Grand Gulch and Canyonlands National Park. Corrugated gray, another popular style, also pops up at a couple of sites in this book. Less common styles include red-on-orange, black-on-orange, and black-on-red.

Other crafts include woven cloth, bone whistles, dice made of horn, stone tobacco pipes, and necklaces and pendants made from wood, bones, snail shells, lignite, turquoise, and hematite. Ancestral Pueblo artisans also made jewelry out of seashells acquired through trade. Tiny copper bells from Mexico have been found at many ruins as well.

In warm weather men wore breechcloths, women wore aprons, and everybody wore sandals made of woven Yucca cord. In winter, shoulder robes made from deer and elk hides helped ward off the cold. Turkey feathers were used to make robes and blankets.

Archaeologists and others have discovered many additional particulars about the Ancestral Pueblo people. In many places, especially in the vicinity of large, sophisticated communities such as those in and around Chaco Canyon, the Native Americans built elaborate networks of roads connecting one settlement to another.

In many places, Ancestral Pueblo people constructed round stone towers several stories high. The towers contained separate rooms and little windows for peering outside. Theories about towers include their use as forts, lookout posts, signaling stations, and ceremonial structures. Some of the best-preserved towers today are at Hovenweep National Monument in Utah.

The Ancestral Pueblo people attached cradleboards to infants in order to flatten the backs of their skulls. This practice, done to achieve what was considered an aesthetically pleasing look, continued into historic times.

Many Native Americans domesticated dogs, and Ancestral Pueblo people were no exception. Two particularly well-preserved canines were excavated from a place called White Dog Cave. The dog for whom the cave was named was about the size of a collie and had long whitish fur. The other was about the size of a terrier and had black and white fur. In addition to making good pets, the animals probably warned the Native Americans of intruders and helped keep the cave clean of food scraps. Some dogs may have even become food themselves.

By A.D. 1300 agricultural, commercial, social, and religious patterns broke down, and population throughout the Ancestral Pueblo world declined dramatically. This decline could have been caused by adverse climate such as drought, more people living on one piece of land than the area could support, intraregional conflict, or pressure from outside groups. Contrary to popular belief, the Ancestral Pueblo people did not simply vanish. Archaeologists are now quite certain they migrated south and southeast. Many resettled in the Rio Grande Valley of New Mexico.

Descendants of the Ancestral Pueblo people still occupy nineteen pueblos in New Mexico and twelve Hopi pueblos in Arizona. Some of the best-known living pueblos include the settlements of Hopi, Zuni, Taos, and Acoma. These communities share many superficial similarities such as architecture and farm life, but they vary greatly in language, religion, and philosophy. With their traditional pueblo-style architecture and residents in native garb, the villages have also become popular tourist attractions, although the Native Americans limit access to their homes.

You may want to see some of the ruins Ancestral Pueblo people left behind. In New Mexico, some of the best-known archaeological regions include Chaco Culture National Historical Park and Bandelier National Monument. In Arizona, Canyon de Chelly National Monument and Navajo National Monument top the list. Utah's Hovenweep National Monument and Colorado's Mesa Verde National Park are also quite spectacular. The ancient buildings at these sites are among the largest and best-preserved Native American ruins north of the Mexican border. As a result, they are highly protected and have become popular tourist attractions. Most are easily accessible, although a few specific ruins, such as Yapashi Pueblo in Bandelier National Monument and the Kiet Siel cliff dwelling in Navajo National Monument, provide good opportunities for backcountry hiking. Of course, there are also thousands of less-known ruins throughout the Ancestral Pueblo world, a few of which I describe in the following pages.

25 Nankoweap (Grand Canyon)

Type of hike: Backpack.
Total distance: About 28 miles (from end of Forest Road 610).
Difficulty: Strenuous.
Topo maps: USGS quads—Nankoweap Mesa, Point Imperial (Nankoweap Trail not shown on topo maps).
Ruin coordinates: N36° 18' 00" W111° 51' 49".
Administration: Grand Canyon National Park.

Given the size of the Grand Canyon, its location in the Ancestral Pueblo region, and the fact that it contains more than 2,000 archaeological sites, one might expect to find an abundance of large cliff dwellings within Grand Canyon National Park. It may be somewhat disappointing, then, to learn that really big rock houses don't exist within the park. There are, however, numerous granaries in the cliffs, including a remarkably well-preserved structure near the mouth of Nankoweap Creek.

Nestled in an enclave 500 feet above the Colorado River, the ruin contains four perfectly intact rooms and the crumbling remains of a fifth. Each tiny room shares a wall with its neighbor, but there is no access from one chamber to another. The little doorways leading into the rooms still have wooden lintels at the top, an architectural feature that added enough structural stability to help keep the entrances intact for 900 years.

As with all granaries, this one was used to store food. Douglas W. Schwartz, an archaeologist who investigated the site in 1960, found corncobs, a pumpkin seed, and a pumpkin shell inside the ruin. The local inhabitants grew these crops on small plateaus above Nankoweap Creek between A.D. 1050 and 1150. On many of the plateaus, the residents aligned boulders to create "dams" up to 50 feet long that diverted water onto their fields.

In addition to the five-room granary, you will see a couple of other small cliff dwellings nearby and, if you look around a lot, other types of ruins. Schwartz documented nearly fifty archaeological sites throughout Nankoweap Canyon, including a petroglyph site and thirty-four pueblo-type house clusters. The house count led him to estimate the local population at about 900.

The entire Grand Canyon was occupied by Ancestral Pueblo people from roughly A.D. 700 to 1200. The population peaked during the Middle Pueblo Period, which coincides with the construction of the Nankoweap cliff dwelling.

How to get there: The easiest way to reach this cliff dwelling is to take a 52-mile rafting or kayaking trip down the Colorado River and put ashore at Nankoweap Creek. In fact, many river runners on commercial tours or with private permits do just that. If you don't have a boat, you must hike the longest, most difficult trail in the Grand Canyon, the Nankoweap Trail.

The Nankoweap Trail starts at the north rim and drops 4,840 feet over a

The Colorado River can be seen from the Nankoweap cliff dwelling.

Nankoweap (Grand Canyon)

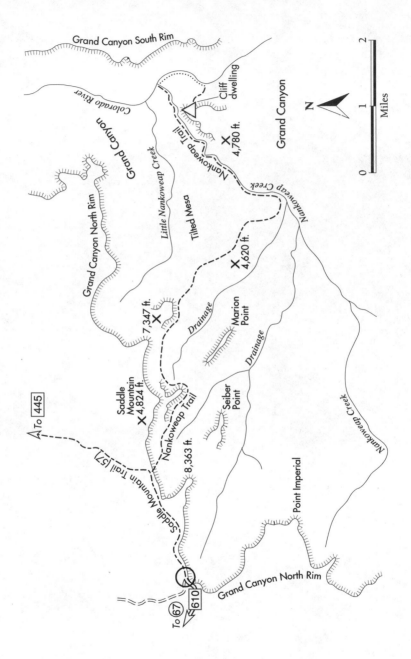

distance of 11 miles to the Colorado River. If that's not enough, you must hike an additional 3 miles to reach the trailhead, bringing the total one-way distance to 14 miles. One of the least-used paths in the park, the Nankoweap Trail is rough and rocky and can at times be visually difficult to follow. The

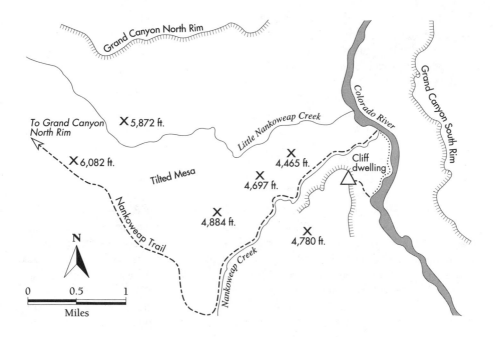

trip also requires driving a considerable distance on graded dirt roads to reach the trailhead.

You cannot hike the Nankoweap Trail in a day, so you must get a permit from the Park Service to camp at least one night, if not two or three. Write to Backcountry Office, Grand Canyon National Park, P.O. Box 129, Grand Canyon, AZ 86023–0129 and ask for a trip planning packet and permit request form. Permits are issued on a first-come, first-served basis, and requests cannot be made more than five months in advance. The north rim of the Grand Canyon is closed in winter.

There are two ways to reach the Nankoweap Trailhead. The first way is to take Arizona 67 south from Jacob Lake. Then, a couple of miles before reaching the entrance to Grand Canyon National Park, turn left (west) onto unpaved Forest Road 611. Drive about a mile, then turn right (south) onto FR 610 and continue roughly 12 miles to the Saddle Mountain Trailhead (Trail 57) at the end of the road. In good weather, you could drive FR 610 in a regular car, but a high-clearance vehicle would be better. Then hike about 3 miles east along Trail 57 to the Nankoweap Trailhead at the rim of the canyon. I took this route and can say that while it is very scenic—with aspen groves and deer galore—the hiking part is relatively difficult with an elevation change of 1,160 feet, which will boost the total elevation change of your trip to 6,000 feet.

The second way to reach the Nankoweap Trailhead is from the north by taking unpaved FR 445 through House Rock Valley. This road will also take you to a trailhead of the Saddle Mountain Trail, but this trailhead is at the *opposite* end of the trail from the one at the end of FR 610. From this trailhead, hike 3.5 miles southwest along Trail 57 to the Nankoweap Trailhead. If you take this route, you'll spend more time driving on a dirt road and hike 0.5 mile farther. However, the elevation change while on foot is only 840 feet—which would bring the total elevation change of your trip to 5,680 feet—and it's stretched out over a slightly longer distance. You may appreciate the gentler incline on the return trip.

From the Nankoweap Trailhead, just follow the rugged path down about 11 miles to the Colorado River. Numerous cairns along the trail will help you find your way. Major landmarks will be Marion Point, followed by Tilted Mesa, then Nankoweap Creek, and finally the Colorado River. From the trailhead to Tilted Mesa, the elevation change is relatively mild. After Tilted Mesa, the trail takes a major plunge down to Nankoweap Canyon.

When you reach the Colorado River, turn around and look up in the cliffs to your left (downriver side of Nankoweap Creek) and you'll spot the ruin. There are several trails leading from Nankoweap Creek up to the granary. They all start out fine but get more faint as they approach the dwelling, and near the end they disappear completely. A much more established trail, the one used by most river runners, begins at the Colorado River about a mile downriver from Nankoweap Creek.

If you don't want to take the Nankoweap Trail all the way to the bottom of the Grand Canyon in one day, there are flat camping spots with great views above Marion Point and at Tilted Mesa. The only drawback at these places is that the ground is too hard for tent stakes, so you'll want a dome-type tent that can stand up without being tied down. The point where the trail enters Nankoweap Canyon—just a few miles short of the Colorado—would also be a nice place to spend a night. Camping is "at large," meaning you do not have to sleep in designated sites.

Each hiker in your group will need 4 to 7 liters of water per day. The only permanent water sources are Nankoweap Creek and the Colorado River. Sometimes there is a seep in the rocks along the trail above Marion Point, but don't count on it. Even if you see water there on the way down, it may not be running on the way up. Since the only reliable sources are at the bottom of the canyon, it is highly recommended that you cache water bottles along the trail on the way down so you do not have to carry so much weight on the way up.

The air temperature at the Grand Canyon ranges from freezing cold to blazing hot, depending on the elevation and time of year. Call the backcountry office at (520) 638-7875 before you go and listen to the recorded weather information.

Utah

26 Hammond Canyon

Type of hike:	Day hike, out-and-back.
Total distance:	About 9 miles.
Difficulty:	Strenuous.
Topo maps:	USGS quads—Kigalia Point, Cream Pots (Hammond Canyon Trail not shown on topo maps).
Ruin coordinates:	N37° 41' 54" W109° 45' 02".
Administration:	Manti-La Sal National Forest.

The search for prehistoric cliff dwellings doesn't usually present much opportunity to venture into the high country, but here's a trek that will take you upward of 8,000 feet. On a dirt road and later on a hiking trail, you'll pass through groves of quaking aspen, stands of towering pines, and lush green meadows before reaching a remarkably well-preserved ruin in Hammond Canyon in Manti-La Sal National Forest.

The Three Fingers Ruin, as it is called, is located 500 feet above the bottom of the canyon. James H. Gunnerson, who conducted an archaeological survey of the area in 1959, determined that the dwelling had nine rooms when it was built between A.D. 900 and 1200 by Native Americans affiliated with the Mesa Verde branch of the Ancestral Pueblo people.

Today, four of the original nine rooms remain quite intact. One of them is a 17-foot-long square "living room" with walls as high as the average person can reach. Half of the big room was once two stories high, but the floor between the stories is now gone. The rear wall contains geometric incised-line petroglyphs.

The other three rooms are round and very tiny. The smaller rooms all look like granaries, although Gunnerson only identified one of them as a storage facility. Smoke-blackened ceilings in the other two small rooms provide evidence that, as cramped as they might appear to modern Americans, they functioned as living quarters.

All the rooms have small square openings in front that look a lot like windows. However, they are actually doors, even the ones located well above the ground. If you want true windows, and also great views up and down Hammond Canyon, peer through the two tiny loopholes in the main room.

There are at least twenty archaeological sites in Hammond Canyon, half of which are cliff dwellings. That may seem like a lot, but the area actually had relatively little prehistoric occupation compared to surrounding areas in Manti-La Sal National Forest.

The patchwork of forest and meadows near the rim of Hammond Canyon, which you will drive through on the way to the trailhead, contains as many deer as you're likely to find anywhere in the country. You can get great photographs with a telephoto lens just by rolling down your car window. I also saw two elk near the trailhead and bear tracks at the bottom of Hammond Canyon.

Hammond Canyon

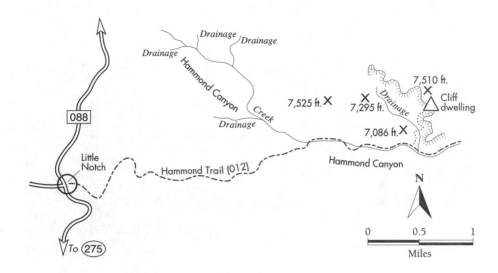

How to get there: This trip includes about 13 miles of driving on a dirt road that in some spots requires high clearance. After that, you must hike about 4.5 miles (one way). The first 2 miles or so drop 1,500 feet, and the total elevation change is 1,900 feet. The hike follows an established trail, except for the last 0.25 mile, which is a steep climb up the canyonside to reach the ruin.

From the junction of Utah 275 and 261, west of Blanding, head northwest on UT 275, toward Natural Bridges National Monument. After driving less than 0.5 mile, veer right onto Forest Road 088, an unpaved road that will take you up to the high country of Manti-La Sal National Forest.

Drive on FR 088 for about 13 miles to a place called Little Notch, which is located in a meadow at 8,240 feet elevation. It's marked with a sign. This is where you will park. The Little Notch area also makes a nice campsite if you arrive late in the day and decide to begin your hike the following morning.

At Little Notch, a smaller dirt road crosses FR 088 (at this writing the USDA Forest Service was considering turning the smaller dirt road into a hiking trail to prevent people from driving on it, which would make it the trailhead for the Hammond Canyon Trail). Walk east along the smaller road for 0.25 mile or so, then onto the Hammond Canyon Trail (Trail 012). Trail 012 starts out easy enough, then suddenly drops 1,500 feet to the bottom of Hammond Canyon. Once at the bottom, however, the trail becomes easy again. The creek at the canyon bottom usually has water year-round.

Once you reach the creek, continue for another 2 miles or so. Keep an eye on the left (north) side of the canyon. The cliff dwelling is located 500 feet above the creek, about 0.25 mile away from the trail. It is near the

At the Three Fingers Ruin in Hammond Canyon, all the rooms except one served as living quarters.

bottom of a huge sandstone column that juts upward. From the opposite rim of the canyon, far from where you stand now, the column looks like three fingers—hence, the ruin's name. There is no established trail leading up to the dwelling, and the climb is fairly difficult.

27 Cottonwood Canyon

Type of hike:	Day hike, out-and-back.
Total distance:	About 9 miles.
Difficulty:	Strenuous.
Topo maps:	USGS quads—Kanab, Yellow Jacket Canyon.
Ruin coordinates:	N37° 04' 12" W112° 35' 36".
Administration:	Bureau of Land Management.

From 1915 to 1920, a man named Neil M. Judd conducted an archaeological survey that extended from the Grand Canyon north to the Great Salt Lake and from Nevada to the Green River in eastern Utah. One day, while exploring Cottonwood Canyon near the town of Kanab, he came across a particularly large and well-preserved Ancestral Pueblo ruin. So impressed was he with the site that he described it as "the largest Cliff-dweller settlement

Cottonwood Canyon

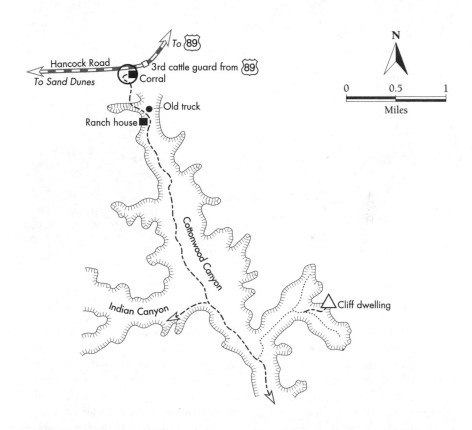

visited by the writer during his archaeological observations north of the Rio Colorado."

Today, the ruin in Cottonwood Canyon is certainly not the largest known cliff dwelling in the huge region covered by Judd, but with nineteen rooms, it's definitely worth the rugged hike required to see it. A half dozen or so of the original nineteen rooms remain quite intact. The ceilings have all fallen down, but most of the walls—which reach nearly 6 feet high in places—appear to be as tall as they were when the dwelling was built. Perfectly preserved windows and loopholes are everywhere, enabling you to gaze inside all of the rooms. While investigating the ruin, it will probably occur to you that the larger chambers appear to have been used for habitation and many of the smaller ones for storage. According to Judd, that was indeed the case. Corn was probably one of the major storage items.

The site also contains a large kiva. Not much is left of the kiva, but you can't miss the giant round hole in the ground where the structure used to be. As mentioned in the Ancestral Pueblo overview, kivas were used as places of work, prayer, schooling, and community gathering.

The largest room in the Cottonwood Canyon cliff dwelling is well preserved.

You won't find much in the way of artifacts at this site, although Judd discovered many things throughout Cottonwood Canyon that provide glimpses into the lives of the Native Americans who lived there. Spindle shafts and whorls made of wood, ceramic, and other materials reveal that the Ancestral Pueblo people spun cotton, and fragments of woven cloth show the results of their work. These Native Americans also wove baskets, made sandals from yucca fiber, and fashioned awls, arrow-shaft smoothers, and other tools from animal bones and horns. Other artifacts recovered from Cottonwood Canyon include stone axes and a perfectly round stone "ball" that may have been used in some sort of kicking game.

How to get there: This trip requires 3.5 miles of easy hiking (one way) followed by about a mile of very difficult hiking. The last mile follows no trail, is heavily overgrown with brush, and has an elevation change of about 700 feet.

The cliff dwelling and the great majority of land covered by this hike are on Bureau of Land Management land. However, the following recommended route passes through a bit of private property owned by Don Riggs, a rancher whose family was among the original founders of Kanab. You must have permission from Mr. Riggs to pass through his property. His number is listed in the Kanab telephone directory. I had no trouble obtaining permission, but if by chance you cannot get permission, you'll have to find an alternate route into Cottonwood Canyon, of which there are many.

From Kanab, drive north on U.S. Highway 89 about 7 miles to Hancock Road. Turn left and continue about 4 miles to a dirt road on the left. For additional reference, the dirt road you are looking for is located *immediately* after the third cattle guard you cross on Hancock Road. From the pavement you will be able to see a small wooden corral about a hundred yards or so down the dirt road. You can park at the corral or on the side of Hancock Road.

Pass through the fence on the opposite (south) side of the corral, then through a second fence to your left just beyond that. Turn right and continue south along a faint dirt road that parallels the barbed-wire fence through which you just passed. The road will lead you into Cottonwood Canyon. The first major landmark you will see when entering the canyon will probably be a large red truck that looks like it hasn't moved in thirty or forty years. Just beyond the truck is a small blue and white ranch house. Head down the canyon (south), past the house, and into the wilderness.

There is no trail at the bottom of Cottonwood Canyon, but there are dirt roads that appear every now and then. When no road is present, just head downstream and you can't go wrong. Some areas are overgrown with thick brush, but overall the going is easy. After hiking 3.5 miles from the corral where you started, turn left (east) into a large (and apparently unnamed) tributary of Cottonwood Canyon. Other than the size of the tributary, which is the largest on the left side of Cottonwood Canyon, there are no outstanding landmarks at this point, so pay close attention to your topographical map.

This is where things start to get difficult, mainly because there is no road or trail leading up the side canyon. While hiking up the tributary, you may find it easier to climb up to the first bench on the left and hike along it rather than push your way through the heavy brush at the very bottom of the canyon. In fact, if you follow the very bottom of the tributary, you will eventually encounter a natural rock "dead end" that will force you to retrace your steps a short distance, then climb up and around it.

After hiking up the tributary for about 0.5 mile, the channel forks in three directions. The cliff dwelling is located at the very top of the middle fork. More specifically, the "middle" fork veers to the right. If you have a compass, the bearing is roughly 60° from where you now stand (the other two forks are at roughly 30° and 90°). At this point you can actually see the enclave that houses the ruin. It's a little less than 0.5 mile away, just beneath the rim of the canyon, facing southeast. However, tall trees in front of the enclave will prevent you from seeing the ruin until you are practically at its front door.

During the final climb up to the dwelling, you cannot follow the stream at the bottom of the canyon because, like the part of the hike you just completed, the canyon boxes up into a natural dead end before you reach the ruin. Instead, climb up the right side of the canyon, about two-thirds of the way up, then turn left and hike toward the ruin along the upper bench. The upper bench on the left side of the canyon may also lead you to the ruin, but I did not try it. Whichever way you go, don't forget that you cannot see the ruin until you are very close to it.

The barbed-wire fence in front of the cliff dwelling keeps out cattle, which in the past destroyed much of this archaeological site.

28 Upper Salt Creek (Canyonlands National Park)

Type of hike:	Backpack, out-and-back.
Total distance:	About 15.5 miles.
Difficulty:	Strenuous.
Topo maps:	USGS quads—Cathedral Butte, South Six-Shooter Peak, Druid Arch, House Park Butte.
Site coordinates:	Big Ruin at N38° 00' 08" W109° 44' 45", All American Man at N38° 02' 04" W109° 44' 53".
Administration:	Canyonlands National Park.

Canyonlands National Park combines opportunities for spectacular backcountry hiking with a chance to see numerous archaeological sites. One of the best places in the park to find both wilderness and prehistoric relics is upper Salt Creek.

The Salt Creek area was occupied by the Mesa Verde branch of the Ancestral Pueblo people primarily between A.D. 1075 and 1150. The large drainage is the only place in the park with both arable land and a perennial water supply. These benefits, combined with the fact that the canyon walls offer protection from the elements and have numerous alcoves suitable for holding cliff dwellings, resulted in a heavier prehistoric occupation of Salt Creek than surrounding areas.

Today, all you have to do to find cliff dwellings and rock art along Salt Creek is keep your eyes open. The more you look around, the more sites you'll find. If you go, make sure you see two particularly interesting sites, the Big Ruin cliff dwelling and the All American Man pictograph.

With twenty-four original structures, most of which appear basically intact, Big Ruin lives up to its name. The dwelling sits high on a rock ledge and is completely inaccessible to hikers, but you can see it just fine from the base of the cliff. The occupants used ropes and ladders to reach their lofty home.

Archaeologists have found the remains of corn and squash inside Big Ruin, which reveals that the occupants made good use of the nearby soil and water. Other artifacts recovered by researchers have included large woven baskets, turkey feather cordage, and cotton cordage. Today, decorated potsherds, arrowheads, and metates and manos can still be seen beneath the ruin.

Though you cannot get very close to this ruin because of its location high in the cliff, the dwelling is so large that it easily fills the frame of a photograph, even if you're standing a good distance away and using an ordinary lens. However, if you want to zoom in on individual rooms and show details such as doors and windows, you'll need a telephoto lens.

A couple of miles down the trail from Big Ruin is one of the most spectacular pictographs you'll find anywhere in the Southwest. Located inside a

Upper Salt Creek (Canyonlands National Park)

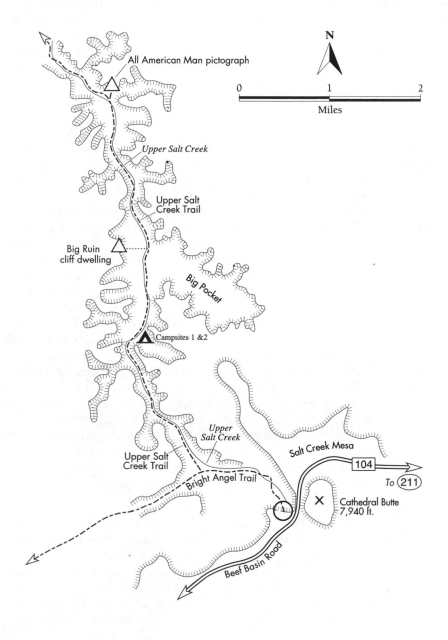

tiny cave along with a small cliff dwelling, the 4-foot-tall picture of a human stands out not for its size but for its color. The Ancestral Pueblo people created the image using red, white, and blue paint. The patriotic appearance of the artwork led to its name, the All American Man.

The pictograph is so striking that many people who see it doubt its authenticity (the register near the site is full of skeptical comments by hikers). Even archaeologists have had their doubts, pointing out that while these Native Americans had a relatively easy time making red and white paint, they are not known to have used blue paint anywhere else and would have had a very difficult time producing it. Researchers responded by taking a very small sample of the blue paint and running some radiocarbon tests on it, which confirmed that the pictograph is indeed of prehistoric origin. Scientists also looked at the blue paint under an electron microscope. They discovered that the "blue" is not blue at all but a gray color made with charcoal. When drawn over the natural orange color of the rock inside the cave, the two hues mix to create the illusion of blue. Furthermore, since modern Americans are accustomed to seeing red, white, and blue—and not red, white, and gray—our brains have a tendency to perceive the color combination with which we are more familiar.

In the center of the All American Man is a large circle that could easily be mistaken for the image's body. Actually, the circle is thought to be a shield. Shielded figures were very common at Ancestral Pueblo sites and also on the Great Plains during the mid 1200s to early 1300s. This period is believed to have been marked by an increased competition for resources, and pictures of shields may have been the Native Americans' way of marking their territory and warning intruders.

The Park Service discourages hikers from climbing up inside the cave where the All American Man is located. Apparently the walls of the cliff dwelling near the pictograph are very unstable, and even small vibrations created by stomping around inside the cave could damage them. That means you must view the rock art from the entrance to the cave, at a distance of about 30 feet. The light inside the cave is fairly dim, even in the middle of the day. If you want a good photograph, pack along a telephoto lens and a flash capable of illuminating an object at 30 feet (the average built-in flash, such as those on point-and-shoot cameras, has a range of about 10 feet). If you don't have a big enough flash, bring a tripod and take a time exposure. Either way, you're going to have to pack some extra weight if you want a decent picture.

How to get there: This trip includes an 18-mile drive on a dirt road that is for the most part graded. However, at a few points a little extra ground clearance will be useful. After that you must hike 5.25 miles (one way) to reach Big Ruin and an additional 2.5 miles to see the All American Man. The first 1.75 miles of the hike drop about 1,000 feet, but after that the route is basically flat. The trail is well established, although in many places it's lined with tall grass that can irritate your legs if you're wearing short pants.

You must have a permit to hike Upper Salt Creek, even if you are just going for a day hike. Call the Park Service at (435) 259-7164 for information on how to obtain day use or overnight permits. Reservations for overnight stays must be made in advance, and you must sleep in a designated campsite.

If you look hard at the red, white, and blue All American Man pictograph, you can see handprints around the prehistoric patriot.

The designated campsites closest to Big Ruin are campsites 1 and 2.

From the junction of U.S. Highway 191 and Utah 211, drive west on UT 211 for about 19 miles to Beef Basin Road (Forest Road 104), which is not paved. Drive on Beef Basin Road for about 18 miles to Cathedral Butte, which is on top of Salt Creek Mesa. Park your vehicle near the Bright Angel Trailhead on the southwest side of Cathedral Butte.

Hike northwest on the Bright Angel Trail. As mentioned, the trail will drop about 1,000 feet in the first 1.75 miles. When you reach the bottom of the canyon, follow the Upper Salt Creek Trail, which continues down the canyon, paralleling the Upper Salt Creek. After hiking about 5 miles from your vehicle, you will reach an area on the right (east) called the Big Pocket, which is a large, open tributary of Salt Creek. At this point, the cliff dwelling becomes easily visible on the left (west) side of the canyon. The ruin sits on a narrow ledge high on a cliff, about 0.25 mile from the trail.

No trail leads from the Upper Salt Creek Trail to the cliff dwelling. If you venture off the beaten path to get a closer look, do your best not to step on the cryptobiotic soil, a black crust containing bacteria that covers much of the ground in Canyonlands National Park. The dark, delicate stuff plays an important role in the ecosystem by helping to stabilize the soil, and if you step on it you will destroy it. A Park Service employee will go over this and other important information when you pick up your permit.

To reach the All American Man, continue north on the Upper Salt Creek Trail, past Big Ruin, for about 2.5 more miles. This brings the total hiking distance from your vehicle to 7.75 miles. The pictograph will be in a tall, narrow "cave" on the right side of the trail. It's hard to see the cave until you get fairly close to it. You will see the small cliff dwelling inside the cave before you see the rock art.

If you're in good shape, it may be possible to hike to the Big Ruin and the All American Man and return to your vehicle in a single day. However, there are so many things to explore along the trail—including caves, natural rock arches, and additional archaeological sites—that you really ought to make it an overnight trip.

29 Moqui Canyon

Type of hike:	Day hike, out-and-back.
Total distance:	About 8.5 miles.
Difficulty:	Strenuous.
Topo map:	USGS quad—Burnt Spring.
Ruin coordinates:	N37° 28' 40" W110° 28' 10".
Administration:	Bureau of Land Management.

Perhaps the most spectacular aspect of Moqui Canyon is the canyon itself. This huge tributary of Glen Canyon features dramatic red-rock scenery strikingly similar to that found at Canyon de Chelly in northern Arizona. However, unlike the large cliff dwellings at the celebrated national monument to the south, any archaeological sites you find in Moqui Canyon are more of a bonus to your hiking experience than the main attraction.

One of the best bonuses I could find in Moqui Canyon was a petroglyph site located inside a long, shallow alcove that once held an Ancestral Pueblo cliff dwelling. The ruins have all but disappeared, but much of the former occupants' artwork can still be seen on the surrounding rocks. Pictures of animals dominate the site, including one very well-preserved bighorn sheep. You'll also find a few images of people, plus a multitude of squiggly lines that defy interpretation.

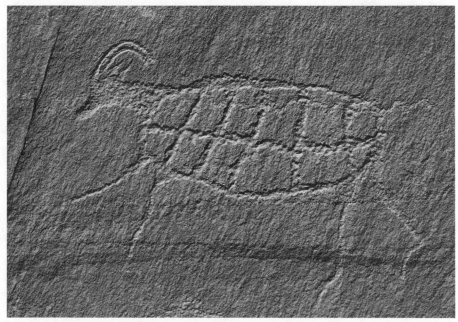

This petroglyph of a bighorn sheep in Moqui Canyon lacks color, but it's cut so deeply into the cliff it stands out anyway. Several boulder metates are located beneath the sheep.

Moqui Canyon

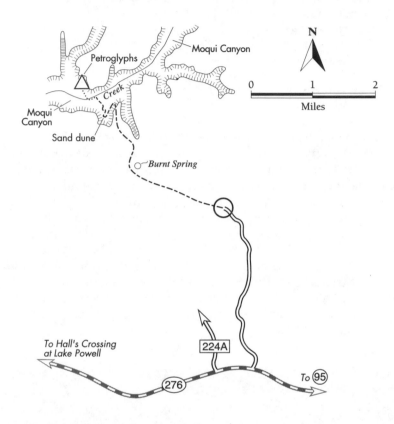

If you look directly below the bighorn sheep, you'll find a boulder covered with a half dozen or so shallow metates. The tools, used to grind corn, are consistent with observations made by archaeologists who surveyed the area more than thirty years ago. "Moqui Canyon, filled over much of its length to a considerable depth with arable alluvial soils, and provided with a plentiful water supply, was no doubt highly attractive to gardeners. In every aspect, Moqui Canyon . . . invited habitation," wrote archaeologist Kent C. Day and others in a 1961 report.

Archaeologists have also determined that the people of Moqui Canyon came primarily from the Mesa Verde region in southwest Colorado. They occupied Moqui Canyon from about A.D. 500 to around 1300.

How to get there: This trip requires at least 3 miles of driving on a poor dirt road, followed by a 4.25-mile hike (one way). Most of the hiking route follows an established trail or undrivable dirt road. The section of hiking trail going from the rim of Moqui Canyon to the bottom drops about 500 feet in about 0.5 mile, and the switchbacks are completely covered by a

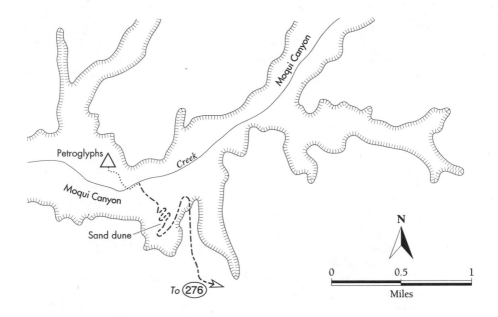

very soft sand slide, a virtual sand dune that has blown over the rim of the canyon.

From the junction of Utah 95 and UT 261 (just west of Blanding), drive west on UT 95 about 8 miles. Turn left on UT 276 and continue southwest about 27.5 miles to a dirt road on the right. The dirt road is not marked, but it is about 0.5 mile before CR 224a, which is marked with a sign. The best thing to do is find CR 224a first, then turn around and drive the opposite direction on the highway (east) for 0.5 mile to the first dirt road on your left (north).

This dirt road winds its way north through the wilderness for roughly 3 miles before it becomes so soft it cannot be driven with most vehicles. The point at which the road becomes the hiking trail may vary depending on current conditions, the type of vehicle you have, and your willingness to press on when the driving becomes difficult. I could only go about 3 miles with a two-wheel drive truck in dry weather.

After reaching this point, hike—or drive if you can—about 3 more miles to the rim of Moqui Canyon. Find the hiking trailhead at the rim, which begins where the road ends. Hike down the switchbacks to the creek at the very bottom of the canyon, a distance of about 1 mile. When you reach the creek, walk downstream (left) about 0.25 mile. The petroglyphs are located inside a long, shallow alcove on the right (north) side of the canyon, just above the canyon bottom. You cannot see the rock art from the streambed. You must climb up to the alcove in order to see them. The best petroglyphs are on the far left side of the alcove, but there are some on the far right as well.

There are countless other archaeological sites in Moqui Canyon. If you decide to hike farther up or down the canyon, just for the fun of it, keep an eye out for additional ruins, petroglyphs, and artifact scatters.

The spelling of the name "Moqui" varies from map to map. One of the most common alternative spellings is "Moki."

30 Grand Gulch (via Collins Canyon)

Type of hike: Day hike, out-and-back.
Total distance: About 8 miles.
Difficulty: Moderate.
Topo map: USGS quad—Red House Spring.
Ruin coordinates: N37° 24' 57" W110° 8' 35".
Administration: Bureau of Land Management.

Here's a cliff dwelling that has just about everything you'd hope to find at a Native American ruin—nicely preserved walls, pottery, rock art, corncobs, stone tools, and even a kiva.

You'll find the ruin after a pleasant hike down Collins Canyon, a tributary of Grand Gulch, and then down the gulch a couple of miles. The ruin sits in what might be described as a "double-decker" enclave. The upper enclave, which holds the main ruin, is completely inaccessible to visitors. However, it's low enough that you can get a good look at the well-preserved walls and intact doors of the cliff dwelling. Two wooden beams in front of the dwelling appear to form banisters, a feature that prompted the site's common name, Banister Ruin. The Ancestral Pueblo people, who built the ruin sometime between A.D. 1060 and 1270, probably used ladders to reach the upper dwelling.

The lower enclave houses an amazingly well-preserved structure that could easily be mistaken for an oven or kiln, but it's actually a kiva. Even the roof, which includes a door for entry through the top, is perfectly intact. A smaller opening near the bottom of the kiva probably served as a ventilator. As mentioned in the Ancestral Pueblo overview, kivas were used as places of work, prayer, schooling, and community gathering.

The Grand Gulch Ancestral Pueblo people made several types of pottery, including a black-on-white style and a corrugated (rough-surfaced) gray ware. You can find sherds of both type lying around the ruin. As mentioned, you should also keep your eyes open for corncobs, small stone tools, and other prehistoric knickknacks.

Faint petroglyphs and pictographs on the cliff are all round the ruin, including a fairly nice broad-shouldered human. I encountered a group of "backpackers"—each of whom had a llama to carry his load—who said they

Grand Gulch (via Collins Canyon)

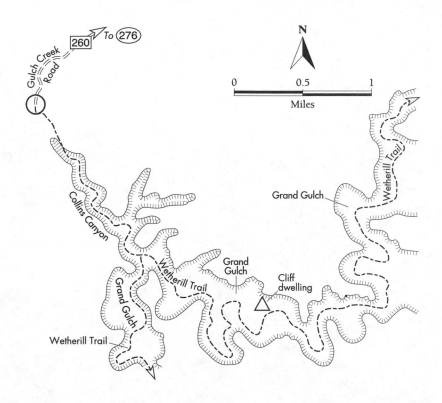

discovered an even better display of petroglyphs downstream from the ruin a bit on one of the upper benches of the north side of the canyon.

One of the best vantage points from which to take a photo of Banister Ruin is on the opposite rim of the canyon, shooting down on the cliff dwelling with a telephoto lens. To reach the opposite rim you have to walk downstream from the ruin a hundred yards or so, climb up the rocks, then head back toward the dwelling.

Grand Gulch contains a wealth of archaeological resources in addition to the places described in this and the following site description. The number of additional ruins and rock art sites you discover is entirely a function of how much you look around. If you're planning a hike anywhere in Grand Gulch, it is highly recommended that you schedule extra time to venture up the side canyons and generally explore the place rather than blowing down the main trail as fast as you can.

How to get there: This trip includes about a 6-mile drive on a poor dirt road followed by about 4 miles of hiking (one way) on established trails. The total elevation change is about 200 feet, the bulk of which occurs in the first 1.6 miles. At certain times of the year you may get your boots wet crossing

123

The Banister Ruin is located inside an inaccessible enclave, and the kiva is directly below it.

back and forth across the creek at the bottom of Grand Gulch.

From the junction of Utah 95 and UT 261 (just west of Blanding), drive west on UT 95 about 8 miles. Turn left on UT 276 and continue southwest about 6.5 miles to Gulch Creek Road (CR 260), which will be on the left and marked with a sign. Take CR 260 for about 6 miles to a trailhead at the top of Collins Canyon.

Follow the hiking trail down Collins Canyon about 1.6 miles to the Wetherill Trail at the bottom of Grand Gulch. When you reach the gulch, take good note of your surroundings so you can find the junction on your way back. Be careful: Numerous tributaries lead into Grand Gulch, and on the way back they all tend to look the same. Hike up (left) the gulch and continue for another 2.4 miles. The ruin will be on the left side of the canyon. You can't miss it.

When you reach the ruin, take special care not to disturb the kiva. If you want to see the roof, do not climb on top of the fragile structure. Instead, climb on top of the large boulder conveniently located just to the right of the kiva and look down.

31 Grand Gulch (via Todie Canyon)

Type of hike:	Day hike, out-and-back.
Total distance:	About 8 miles.
Difficulty:	Moderate, with one short but difficult stretch.
Topo map:	USGS quad—Cedar Mesa North.
Ruin coordinates:	N37° 28' 52" W109° 58' 54".
Administration:	Bureau of Land Management.

One of the greatest pleasures of hiking to any Native American ruin is discovering sites along the way that you never even set out to find. The 4-mile trek to Split Level Ruin in Grand Gulch Primitive Area provides abundant opportunities for such experiences.

As soon as you begin the hike you start discovering things. Practically every south- or southeast-facing enclave, alcove, and cave in the canyonside holds a granary or small cliff dwelling. If you wander off the main trail a bit, you can find all kinds of rock art, including one site with numerous red pictographs of human hands.

Of course, there's also the final destination. The ruin is built on two natural terraces, each at a different elevation (thus, the name: Split Level Ruin). Both rooms have intact walls all around, and large wooden ceiling beams are still in place. In some spots the main beams support smaller poles, sticks, and mud. The site is preserved exceptionally well. Smaller rooms and storage facilities are also scattered about the site.

Grand Gulch (via Todie Canyon)

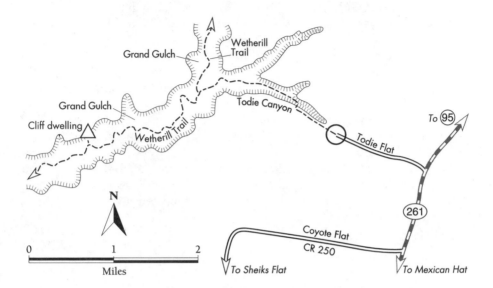

You'll find about as many artifacts at Split Level Ruin as you would at Banister Ruin described in the previous pages. The dwelling was built during the same period as Banister Ruin, sometime between A.D. 1060 and 1270.

How to get there: This trip includes 1.2 miles of driving on a poor dirt road followed by about 4 miles of hiking (one way). Overall the hike is rated as moderate, but there is one short but difficult section that drops about 200 feet into a canyon. The difficult part follows a marked route, not a trail, and is extremely rocky. The elevation change for the entire hike is about 350 feet, which means that except for that initial drop into the canyon, the route is basically flat.

From the town of Mexican Hat near the Utah-Arizona border, drive north on Utah 261 about 26 miles to a dirt road that turns left (west) off of the pavement and onto Todie Flat. The road is not marked, but it's the first dirt road north of dirt County Road 250, which is marked with a sign and goes to Coyote Flat. Take this road about 1.2 miles to a trailhead and small parking area at the top of Todie Canyon. Hikers are asked to sign a registration form and pay a small user fee at the trailhead voluntarily.

The trail begins easily enough by paralleling the south rim of Todie Canyon. The path disappears from time to time, but the route is well marked with cairns and generally easy to follow. After about 0.5 mile, the trail suddenly turns right and drops straight down into Todie Canyon. As mentioned, things get rough at this point and stay rough until you reach the bottom of

The left half of this photo shows the two rooms that gave Split Level Ruin its name.

the canyon. In very cold weather, ice and snow on the rocks can make the descent into the gorge fairly hazardous.

Once you reach the bottom, continue down Todie Canyon for about 1.5 miles until you reach the Wetherill Trail at the bottom of Grand Gulch. Head downstream (left) for about 2 more miles to Split Level Ruin, which will be on the right, alongside the trail.

The Wetherill Trail is fairly well established, but if you get confused by all the tributaries and side canyons during any point of the hike, just remember to follow downstream the largest waterway you can find and you'll eventually end up at Split Level Ruin. Also, as discussed earlier, you may discover many other ruins on the way to Split Level Ruin. You may even mistake one or two of the larger cliff dwellings near the trail for your final destination. To avoid mistakes, keep three things in mind: (1) Split Level Ruin is relatively large and well-preserved; (2) It is well within view of the main trail at the bottom of Grand Gulch; and (3) It is easily accessible from the main trail (no rock climbing required).

New Mexico

32 Bandelier National Monument

Type of hike:	Backpack, out-and-back.
Total distance:	About 21 miles.
Difficulty:	Strenuous.
Topo maps:	USGS quads—Frijoles, Cochiti Dam.
Site coordinates:	Yapashi Pueblo at N35° 45' 39" W106° 18' 52", Stone Lions at N35° 45' 55" W106° 19' 07", Painted Cave at N35° 43' 19" W106° 19' 17".
Administration:	Bandelier National Monument.

Of all the major archaeological parks in New Mexico, only Bandelier National Monument offers opportunities for true backcountry hiking. Beyond the visitor center, and easily accessible ruins near it, lie 37,000 acres of wilderness, and just about every wild acre contains evidence of prehistoric occupation.

Three of the most interesting hiking destinations in Bandelier are Yapashi Pueblo, the Stone Lions shrine, and the Painted Cave pictograph site. Collectively, these sites date back to about A.D. 1200 when Ancestral Pueblo people occupied the region. However, as you will soon learn, the sites continue to be used today by modern Pueblo Indians.

Yapashi Pueblo, located nearly 6 miles down the trail from the visitor center, is the largest unexcavated pueblo in Bandelier. A surface survey determined the ground floor had 350 rooms, and some believe the pueblo may have had up to four stories. The site also has six kivas, four within the pueblo and two just outside. Yapashi was occupied between A.D. 1200 and 1475 and is thought to have housed up to 500 people.

Today, a few of the walls still stand up to 4 feet high, but for the most part the pueblo looks like a big pile of rubble. The walls are not the main attraction, though. As you wander around the site, your eyes will be drawn to the massive collection of ceramics and lithics scattered on the ground. The pottery consists mostly of plainware, although some decorated sherds, including small black-on-white pieces, can be found. The lithics include all sorts of small, crudely shaped objects made of shiny black obsidian and other stones. It's hard to say if any given rock was used for cutting, scraping, and chipping or created as a by-product when larger tools were made.

According to traditional stories, the ancestors of modern Native Americans living at Cochiti Pueblo, located just south of Bandelier, built Yapashi Pueblo. Evidence for the Cochiti-Yapashi connection includes the fact that black-on-white pottery made at the living pueblo is very similar to the ceramics found at the prehistoric one. However, some archaeologists disagree with the Cochiti about their heritage. The Keresan language spoken at Cochiti is quite different from the language spoken at neighboring pueblos, indicating the Cochiti are relatively recent arrivals to the area.

The name "Yapashi" is derived from the Keresan word "Yapashenye," which means "sacred enclosure." This is a reference to the Stone Lions shrine

Bandelier National Monument

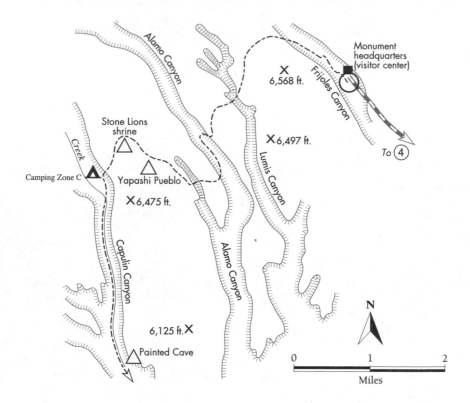

located about 0.5 mile down the trail.

The Stone Lions shrine consists of two mountain lions, each about 6 feet long, carved into volcanic tuff boulders. The two animals lie side by side, facing east, with their tails extended. A wall made of boulder slabs encircles the lions, creating the "enclosure" considered sacred by Native Americans. The statues have suffered considerable damage by vandals who have used everything from crowbars to dynamite, but you can still make out the lions pretty well, especially their hind legs and tails.

The lions, which lay in a crouched position, look as if they are about to pounce on something. It should come as no surprise, then, that the site is a hunting shrine. In fact, Edgar L. Hewett, who studied this and nearby sites around the turn of the century, referred to the Stone Lions as "the most important hunting shrine in the entire pueblo region."

The Stone Lions were made by prehistoric Native Americans, but residents of Cochiti Pueblo still visit the shrine. Young men from Zuni Pueblo, located 400 miles away, also used to make pilgrimages on foot to the Stone Lions as part of a rite of passage into manhood.

Interestingly, old photos of the Stone Lions show a ring of deer and elk antlers surrounding the statues. The antlers are no longer there.

About 4 miles down the trail from Stone Lions you will find one of the most spectacular rock art sites in this book, the Painted Cave. The cave, actually an alcove about a hundred feet long, contains a wildly animated gallery of pictographs painted in red, white, and black. The pictures include kachinas, kachina masks, shield figures, handprints, horses, a giant elk, feathered serpents, mean-looking dogs flashing big white teeth, a human holding a kangaroolike animal on a leash, a six-pointed star, a couple of Christian churches complete with crosses and steeples, the New Mexico state symbol (the sun that appears on the state flag, license plates, and state highway signs), a giant monster that bears a strong resemblance to Godzilla, and all kinds of abstractions and geometric patterns.

Obviously, not all of these images are prehistoric. The horses and churches were drawn sometime after the Spaniards arrived in New Mexico in 1540. Other historic pictures include the elk, dogs, six-pointed star, most of the black paintings, and most of the more realistic drawings, including many of the kachinas. Everything else, including most of the simpler images in red and white, predate the arrival of Europeans.

As with the Stone Lions, the Painted Cave was and continues to be an important shrine for the Cochiti. Some remains of a cliff dwelling can be found below the cave, but the overall site was not used for habitation.

The Painted Cave is located about 50 feet above the floor of Capulin Canyon and is not accessible. You can see the large pictographs clearly from below with the naked eye, but photography from such a distance is challenging. Because of the long hike, I opted not to pack a telephoto lens. This was a big mistake, and if you want good pictures, you should bring a big lens that will enable you to zoom in on individual paintings inside the cave.

I encountered a black bear and her cub about a mile north of the Painted Cave. The younger animal, cute as a teddy bear, shot straight up a tree while the mother paced around nervously at its base. It was a magnificent sight, not to mention a frightening reminder that you should exercise proper bear etiquette at Bandelier, including hanging your packs high in a tree during the night.

I also spotted deer, and elk droppings are everywhere at Bandelier.

How to get there: This trip includes roughly 10.5 miles of hiking (one way) on well-established trails. The trails dip in and out of five different canyons that have a combined elevation change (not a net elevation change) of roughly 2,150 feet. The elevation change between canyons and along the bottom of canyons is not very great.

You must obtain a permit to camp or backpack overnight, but reservations are not required. Simply show up at the visitor center before beginning your hike and tell the staff where you're going. The center, located just off New Mexico 4 in Frijoles Canyon, is open seven days a week except Christmas and New Year's Day. Summer hours are 8:00 A.M. to 6:00 P.M., and winter hours are 8:00 A.M. to 4:30 P.M.

Park in the lot reserved for backcountry hikers just south of the visitor center, on the opposite side of Frijoles Creek. Find the trailhead with a sign giving the mileage to Yapashi Ruin (5.7 miles) and Painted Cave (10.4 miles).

The two animals at the Stone Lions shrine face left. The heads are hard to make out, but the tails are a bit easier to see.

Follow the trail up the southeast side of Frijoles Canyon to the rim. You can see numerous cliff dwellings on the opposite side of the canyon, near the bottom, as you make the ascent.

At the top of Frijoles Canyon, you will come to a junction. Take the trail that heads southeast directly to Yapashi Pueblo and the Stone Lions. A sign at the junction points the way. In fact, signs are posted at every junction on this hike, making it almost impossible to lose your way.

The trail dips in and out of Lumis Canyon, Alamo Canyon, and a small tributary of Alamo Canyon before reaching Yapashi Pueblo. The first two gorges are marked with signs. Lumis Canyon is no big deal, but Alamo Canyon takes a 600-foot plunge and is the most difficult part of the entire trip.

You'll eventually reach Yapashi Pueblo and, less than 0.5 mile beyond that, the Stone Lions shrine. After the Stone Lions, the trail turns south and drops roughly 700 feet to the bottom of Capulin Canyon. Actually, you catch a bit of Hondo Canyon on the way down before entering Capulin. The climb out of Capulin Canyon on the return trip will be difficult, but it's not quite as difficult as Alamo Canyon because the trail changes elevation more gradually.

At the bottom of Capulin Canyon is Camping Zone C, a cool, shady place with permanent water. This is probably the best spot to spend the night. If you arrive early enough, you can set up camp, then take an easy 2.25-mile walk down Capulin Canyon and see the Painted Cave. If you arrive late in the afternoon, save the cave for the following morning.

As mentioned, there is permanent water in Capulin Canyon, but it contains the parasite *Giardia lamblia* and must be treated accordingly. No other canyons on this trip, not even Alamo Canyon, have reliable water.

The Gallina Phase

The term "Gallina Phase" refers to a cultural phenomenon that occurred between A.D. 1050 and 1300 in a relatively small area within the Ancestral Pueblo region. Some archaeologists lump the Gallina Indians in with their Pueblo neighbors, but there are enough differences between the two groups that most recognize the Gallina as a separate culture.

The Gallina region is centered in northern New Mexico around the Gallina River, a tributary of the Chama River. The area extends north to the Jicarilla Apache Reservation, south to the San Pedro and Jemez Mountains, east to the Chama River, and west to the Continental Divide.

Like the Ancestral Pueblo people, the Native Americans of the Gallina Phase grew corn, supplemented their cultivated diet with wild foods, built houses of stone, held ceremonies in kivas, and made black-on-white pottery. However, the *way* they did certain things set them apart.

As far as Gallina pottery goes, it is known not so much for its color as for its unique shape. Many of the ceramic vessels have a characteristic cone-shaped bottom. When used for cooking, the pots' pointed bottoms helped them remain upright while sitting in a bed of ash.

The pots resemble those made by Native Americans in eastern Colorado and western Nebraska, opening up the possibility that the Gallina people came from those areas. If so, they may be related to the Fremont culture in Utah, who also originated in the plains. However, the nonpointed, black-on-white decorated wares resemble those made by the Ancestral Pueblo people of the San Juan River area.

Interestingly, archaeologists have found almost no foreign-made pottery at Gallina sites, suggesting the Gallina were a very isolated group and did not trade much with the Pueblo Indians around them.

Many other Gallina artifacts, including knives, axes, adzes, and tobacco pipes, are also very distinctive and help set the culture apart.

Architecturally speaking, many Ancestral Pueblo settlements contain large clusters of stone rooms, often several stories high. Gallina pueblos and cliff dwellings, on the other hand, rarely contained more than two rooms connected together. The total number of rooms in one village could be as high as twenty, but individual rooms were for the most part separate structures. Because of this, most Gallina "pueblos" cannot truly be defined as such.

The quality of Gallina masonry tends to be poorer than that of the Ancestral Pueblo people. However, what the Gallina Indians lacked in craft they made up in bulk. Their walls are unusually thick, averaging 1 to 1.5 meters in width and in some cases reaching 6 feet.

Another defining trait of Gallina architecture is the tower. Located on cliff edges, sharp ridges, and other prominent points, the towers stand up to 30 feet high and are either round or square in shape. It is believed they functioned as lookout towers from which to watch for enemies or as signaling stations. At least one researcher raised the possibility that multiple towers worked together to form communication networks, much like the Hohokam fortified hilltops may have done. Some towers also served as living quarters, perhaps for the local war chief, and some may have functioned as granaries.

The Gallina people also made pithouses, which often existed alongside their stone structures.

Little is known about the Gallina Phase, including what happened to the Gallina people after the fourteenth century. No living Pueblo Indians recognize the Gallina people as their ancestors.

Only one Gallina ruin, the Nogales Cliff House, is described in this book. However, it's an interesting ruin and contains many features typical of the Gallina Phase.

33 Spring (Nogales) Canyon

Type of hike: Day hike, out-and-back.
Total distance: About 1.5 miles.
Difficulty: Easy.
Topo maps: USGS quads—Llaves, Cañada Ojitos (hiking trail not shown on topo maps).
Ruin coordinates: N36° 24' 35" W106° 52' 42".
Administration: Santa Fe National Forest.

If you're up for a short but beautiful hike that ends at a neat little cliff dwelling, take a walk up Spring Canyon (aka Nogales Canyon) in Santa Fe National Forest.

The trail follows the bottom of the canyon, where a creek and tall pines create a lush, shady setting. Then it's straight up the side of the canyon to see a ruin known as the Nogales Cliff House. The dwelling, hidden behind the tall trees, sits high in an enclave that would require some pretty serious rock climbing to reach. From below, however, you get a good look at a tall, square tower and intact walls punctured by a doorway and a couple of little windows.

The surrounding slopes contain forty or fifty additional rooms, none of which are very well preserved. Only two rooms in the entire site, the main cliff dwelling and a crumbling structure directly beneath it, were used for habitation. All the others were storage facilities. As with all Gallina settlements, no more than two rooms in the settlement were connected.

While the Nogales Cliff House contains many features typical of the Gallina Phase, it is the only cliff dwelling in the region with any rooms for habitation and, therefore, the only ruin that fits a true definition of a cliff dwelling. All other Gallina "cliff dwellings" were used as granaries. Tree-ring

Spring (Nogales) Canyon

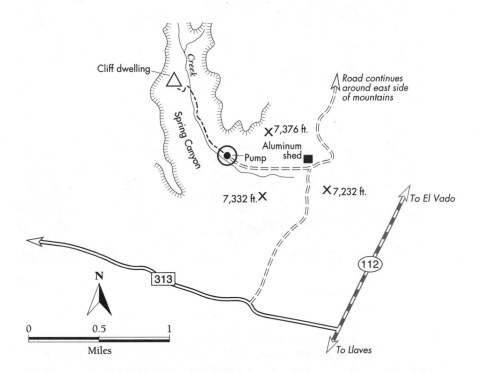

Cliff dwelling

Creek

Spring Canyon

Road continues
around east side
of mountains

X 7,376 ft.

Aluminum
shed

Pump

7,332 ft. X

X 7,232 ft.

To El Vado

313

112

N

0   0.5   1

Miles

To Llaves

samples extracted from wooden beams used in the construction of the dwelling helped date the site to the mid 1200s.

Near the cliff dwelling are some interesting pictographs that you could easily miss. About a hundred yards down the trail from the main part of the ruin, just above the trail, are four white pictures painted onto the rocks. The images look a lot like geese but actually are thought to represent great blue herons. For whatever it's worth, the paint consists of a mixture of organic material and urine. This is actually not a unique formula, as prehistoric Native Americans often added urine or blood to their paint as a bonding agent.

Also keep an eye out for some black pictographs drawn on the back wall of the room directly beneath the main dwelling. They are not obvious. The pictures are said to include a hummingbird and a sunflower tree.

How to get there: This trip includes about 0.75 mile of driving on a graded dirt road and about 1.5 miles of driving on poor dirt roads. A passenger car could make the trip, but a high-clearance vehicle would do much better. The hike is about 0.75 mile (one way) and follows an established trail. The last 0.25 mile or so climbs about 600 feet, but by the time you work up a sweat you'll already be at the ruin.

The best-preserved rooms in the Nogales Cliff House include a tower, which is shown at the left of the photo.

From New Mexico 112, turn west onto Forest Road 313, which begins about 1 mile north of the community of Llaves. Drive west on FR 313 about 0.75 mile to a sign saying you have entered Santa Fe National Forest. Immediately after entering the forest, turn right onto a smaller dirt road. Follow the smaller road about 1 mile north to an aluminum utility shed that appears to house a pump of some sort. Turn left at the shed, heading west toward the mountains, and continue for a little more than 0.5 mile to the end of the road. A pump at the end of the road is surrounded by a thick steel "fence" painted yellow.

Find the trailhead and hike up Spring Canyon. (Old literature calls the area "Nogales Canyon," but it's marked as Spring Canyon on current USGS topo maps.) The trail will take you all the way to the ruin, and it never forks so you can't go wrong. As mentioned, the first 0.5 mile is very easy. Then it takes a left turn straight up the east side of the canyon for about 0.25 mile to reach the cliff dwelling.

The Mogollon Culture

The Mogollon people lived along the Mogollon Rim and other mountainous areas of eastern Arizona and western New Mexico. Their territory also extended well into the Mexican state of Chihuahua. It is believed the Mogollon developed from local Archaic Indians around A.D. 200

The Mogollon are generally considered the least advanced of all the major prehistoric southwestern cultures, primarily because they relied more on hunting and gathering than did their contemporaries. In fact, in the early centuries of their existence, from A.D. 200 to 1000, the Mogollon obtained more of their diet from wild foods such as deer, antelope, bighorn sheep, rabbits, turkeys, acorns, walnuts, piñon nuts, and prickly pear cactus than from domesticated crops. Their use of more Archaic methods does not necessarily indicate a lack of innovation. Their mountainous homeland was more abundant in wild plants and animals than the relatively dry and desolate areas occupied by surrounding cultures, so they probably didn't see the need to develop agriculture to any great extent. Whatever the reason, the Mogollon lifestyle has earned these Native Americans a reputation as a hearty, rugged people who were more adapted to their natural environment than were the Hohokam, Ancestral Pueblo people, and other neighbors.

The relatively small farms that the Mogollon did cultivate contained the usual triad of corn, beans, and squash, along with cotton. Such gardens were usually located on mesa tops and in cool valleys, where terraces were built to reduce soil erosion and retain moisture. The Mogollon did not build many structures to divert or channel water, although some stone "dams" have been found.

During the early periods of their history, the Mogollon rarely built anything much more sophisticated than a pithouse. However, they made very good ones. Mogollon pithouses were true pithouses, dug deep into the ground so that the sides of the pits functioned as interior walls. Villages were small at first, containing four to fifty pithouses and often a great kiva. The presence of large communal structures in relatively small villages indicates that Mogollon settlements scattered over large areas had close ties and met regularly at central locations.

The early Mogollon were apparently fearful of raids by other foragers, for they built their homes on ridges, hilltops, and other easily defensible sites. Access to villages was often blocked by crudely constructed walls. Later, between A.D. 650 and 850, Mogollon settlements became larger and tended to be located in valleys near their farms, which by that time had also become larger.

The earliest Mogollon pottery was undecorated and had a deep earthy brown or reddish color. Over the centuries the Mogollon experimented with coloration, eventually creating red-on-white ceramics, and then, just prior to A.D. 1000, a black-on-white style similar to that of the Ancestral Pueblo people.

Other notable crafts included beads, bracelets, shell pendants, bone whistles, and large stone tubular pipes with mouthpieces made of bone or wood. Tiny copper bells from Mexico have also been found at Mogollon ruins.

After A.D. 1000 the Mogollon acquired many traits that were contemporaneous with developments in the Ancestral Pueblo region. Architecture became more advanced, and above-ground stone pueblos began appearing everywhere. They were small at first but eventually evolved into large, multistory pueblos with hundreds of rooms. The Mogollon also started building cliff dwellings. Perhaps the best known are those at Gila Cliff Dwellings National Monument, just north of Silver City.

Agriculture had been growing in importance slowly since the culture's beginning, but it didn't really take off until around A.D. 1000. After that time, Mogollon farms grew very large, and they became more sophisticated with innovations such as ditch irrigation.

Another noteworthy development after A.D. 1000 was the creation of a "new" style of pottery. Between A.D. 1050 and 1200 there was a great population boom along the Mimbres River in southwestern New Mexico. From this area came a black-on-white style based on Ancestral Pueblo ceramics but containing a completely original composition of human, animal, and mythical figures. The appearance of Mimbres ceramics is so stunning, and its quality so fine, that it is now considered to be the best-made pottery in the prehistoric Southwest.

After A.D. 1300 the Mogollon population began to decrease, and by A.D. 1400 the Mogollon had completely abandoned their homeland. The abandonment was probably due to the same factors that plagued all major southwestern groups at that time.

Although the Mogollon abandoned their mountainous homelands and underwent many cultural changes, they did not disappear. Their descendants continued to live in other parts of Arizona and New Mexico and were among the first Native Americans in the Southwest to encounter Europeans.

Most descendants of the Mogollon live in the same thirty-one pueblos in New Mexico and Arizona that are currently occupied by descendants of the Ancestral Pueblo people. A possible exception are the Mimbres Mogollon, who may have migrated into Mexico's Sierra Madre Mountains and become the Tarahumara and Western Chihuahua Indians.

34 Saddle Mountain

Type of hike: Day hike, out-and-back.
Total distance: About 1 mile.
Difficulty: Moderate.
Topo maps: USGS quads—Saliz Pass, Blue AZ (Blue AZ overlaps two states but is categorized as a New Mexico map).
Ruin coordinates: N33° 36' 22" W109° 00' 15".
Administration: Located within Apache National Forest, administered by Gila National Forest.

> The (Indians) who were on the top for defense were not hindered in the least from doing us whatever injury they were able. As for myself, they knocked me down to the ground twice with countless great stones which they threw down from above, and if I had not been protected by the very good headpiece which I wore, I think that the outcome would have been bad for me.

Those words were written by the Spanish military commander Francisco Vasquez de Coronado after he and his men attacked the Zuni pueblo of Hawikuh in 1540. This chapter is not about Hawikuh—it's about a Mogollon cliff dwelling 90 miles to the south—but any enemy who approached the dwelling must have had an experience very similar to Coronado's.

The ruin is built into a cliff at the southern edge of Saddle Mountain in the San Francisco Mountains of western New Mexico. By my best estimation, it contains only one large room made by covering the front of a natural enclave with a crudely built masonry wall, which still stands about 7 feet high and 30 feet wide. The wall contains a half-dozen loopholes and a single large opening that probably served as a doorway.

The reason the number of rooms is not certain is that the dwelling is completely inaccessible without rock-climbing gear. You can get close, but you can't go inside. No doubt the Native Americans who built the dwelling used ladders or ropes to access the site. If attacked, all they'd have to do is drop "countless great stones" on the enemy.

C. B. Cosgrove, an archaeologist who investigated the site in 1930, noted the defensive nature of the dwelling. He also noted that twenty-five years earlier some cattlemen entered the ruin and found bows, arrows, and other objects, which led them to conclude the site had served as an armory.

An even earlier rancher is reported to have found small painted tablets arranged in an orderly manner around the walls of the enclave. In addition, Cosgrove found some miniature ceremonial bowls in the ruin. Objects such as these have led some to believe the cliff dwelling served as a shrine or a place for sacrificial offerings. In fact, the archaeologist Walter Hough dismissed the defense theory altogether, claiming in a 1907 report that "there is no reason to believe that the cave was used for other purposes than for sacrificial offerings."

Saddle Mountain

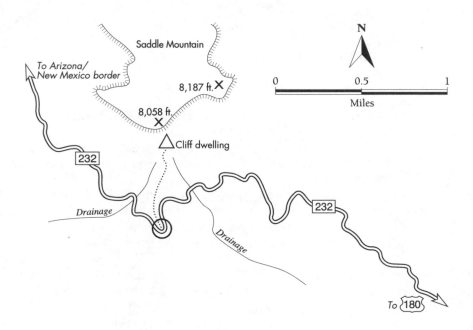

It is also worth noting that Cosgrove found corncobs, two metates, painted and unpainted potsherds, yucca-fiber cordage, human-hair cordage, and a dozen reed cigarettes in the cliff dwelling. The diversity of artifacts from the Saddle Mountain cliff dwelling suggests Native Americans engaged in many different activities at the site, so no single theory about the ruin's function may be correct.

Since you cannot walk right up to the ruin, you'll need a telephoto lens to get a good picture.

How to get there: Fitness experts say a person must elevate his or her heart rate for about twenty minutes before beginning to reap the benefits of aerobic respiration. The Saddle Mountain cliff dwelling is less than 0.5 mile from a dirt road, but if you hike to the ruin, you'll definitely get your work-out. There is no trail, the terrain is rough and rocky, and the elevation change is about 600 feet. Binoculars are helpful for finding the ruin from the road. The trip also includes a 10-mile drive on a graded dirt road.

From the junction of New Mexico 12 and U.S. Highway 180, drive south on US 180 about 5 miles to Forest Road 232, which is unpaved but well-graded. Head west on FR 232 about 10 miles to the southern base of Saddle Mountain. Once there, look in the cliffs near the top of the mountain to see the ruin. It may take awhile to spot, but it's up there.

A nice area to park is at the tip of a large U-turn in the road. From there, scope out what looks like the best route up to the cliff dwelling and start

This cliff dwelling can be found at Saddle Mountain.

climbing. The distance "as the crow flies" is only about 0.25 mile, but your actual hiking route may be twice that.

As mentioned, you can get close to the ruin but you cannot go inside. You will, however, find several ropes dangling from the ruin, which previous hikers have used to climb up into the dwelling. You may be tempted to use the ropes yourself. If so, ask yourself how long they've been there weathering away in the sun, wind, and rain. A month? A year? A decade? You have no idea, and if they break during your climb, you're a long way from help.

35 Middle Fork, Gila River

Type of hike: Day hike, out-and-back.
Total distance: About 3.5 miles.
Difficulty: Moderate.
Topo map: USGS quad—Gila Hot Springs.
Ruin coordinates: N33° 14' 39" W108° 14' 01".
Administration: Gila National Forest.

If you ever hike up the Middle Fork of the Gila River—a beautiful part of the Gila Wilderness inhabited by black bears and bald eagles—you'll find it worth your while to take a short trip up a side canyon to see the remains of an eleven-room Mogollon cliff dwelling.

The best-preserved room consists of a wall 5 feet wide and about 7 feet tall that completely covers the entrance to a natural enclave. A single small doorway provides access into the room. According to C. B. Cosgrove, who studied the site in 1929, the room functioned as a granary.

Another room has a 2-foot-long image of an animal on a wall. The artwork, apparently drawn with charcoal, looks very much like a turtle. However, Cosgrove's report includes his own drawing of the animal, which shows

Middle Fork, Gila River

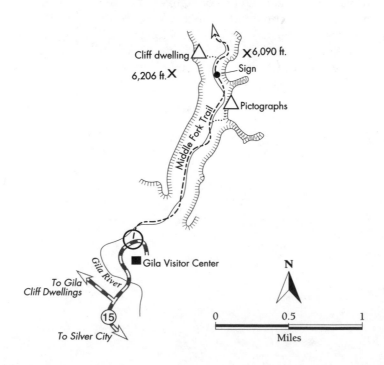

This crumbling pictograph looks like a turtle, but when more intact it looked like a possum or armadillo.

a section of its head that has since disappeared. The missing piece had a snout that makes the creature look more like a possum or armadillo.

You'll also find crumbling remains of additional rooms and a couple of faint red pictographs around the site. All in all, four of the rooms were used for habitation and seven for the storage of food. If you look real hard, you may also find a couple of manos.

About 0.25 mile below the cliff dwelling, high on the opposite side of the canyon, are several red pictographs. They include a large zigzag line, thick rectangular "bars," and tiny human handprints made by children. Interestingly, the Native Americans who made the pictographs did not live in the cliff dwelling upstream. Exactly who did make them is not known for sure, although Polly Schaafsma, a leading authority on rock art, has suggested it may have been the Apaches.

How to get there: The hike to this ruin is only about 1.75 miles (one way) with no significant elevation change. However, it cannot be called an easy hike because the trail crosses the Gila River numerous times. The water level fluctuates, but at certain times of the year it can be high enough to wet your pants pockets. Portions of the trail often get washed out and can be a bit tricky to find. A hiking stick is very helpful for testing the depth of the water in front of you and keeping your balance while crossing the river. Binoculars are useful for viewing the pictographs.

Before you make this trip, you may want to call Gila Cliff Dwellings National Monument at (505) 536-9344 and ask about the current water level in the Middle Fork. This is especially true around March and April when the water level tends to be the highest.

From the visitor center at Gila Cliff Dwellings National Monument, hike up the Middle Fork Trail to a wooden sign saying you've come 1.5 miles. Continue past the sign just a bit, then turn left (west) and bushwhack your way up a small side canyon. The ruin is located where the sloping ground meets the cliff on the north side of the canyon. It's covered with trees and heavy brush, so you won't be able to see it until you are very close.

The pictographs are located downstream from the wooden sign just a bit, way up in the cliff near some "caves" on the east side of the canyon. As mentioned, you should be able to see a large red zigzag design and a rectangular "bar" from the trail. With binoculars, you may even be able to see the handprints. It is possible to get close enough to the rock art for a good picture by climbing up the steep slope on the downstream side of the pictographs.

36 West Slaughter Canyon

Type of hike:	Day hike, out-and-back.
Total distance:	About 13 miles.
Difficulty:	Strenuous.
Topo maps:	USGS quads—Pickett Hill, El Paso Gap.
Pictograph coordinates:	N32° 05' 33" W104° 39' 27".
Administration:	Carlsbad Canyons National Park.

In a remote corner of the Guadeloupe Mountains is West Slaughter Canyon, and in an even more remote corner of West Slaughter Canyon is a seldom-seen rock art site called Upper Painted Grotto.

After a rugged 6.5-mile hike that drops more than 1,000 feet in elevation, you'll come across an alcove roughly 70 feet wide and decorated on the inside with ancient pictographs. Most of the artwork is red, although some drawings are yellow. This multicolored gallery includes zigzag lines, dots arranged in linear patterns, and small circles connected like links in a chain. There are also bull's eyes, something that looks like a cornstalk, round images that resemble spoked wheels, and many other designs. Some of the fainter images could be interpreted as humans, but it's hard to say. A few of the pictographs, including a couple of bull's eyes and a chain of circles, are unusually tiny.

I could find no archaeological reports about this specific site. However, several researchers, including Polly Schaafsma, H. P. Mera, and David Gebhard, have written about what is known today as Lower Painted Grotto, a very similar rock art site in West Slaughter Canyon. Like Upper Grotto, Lower Grotto is located in an alcove about 70 feet wide and contains red and yellow pictographs (along with black and white ones), some of which

West Slaughter Canyon

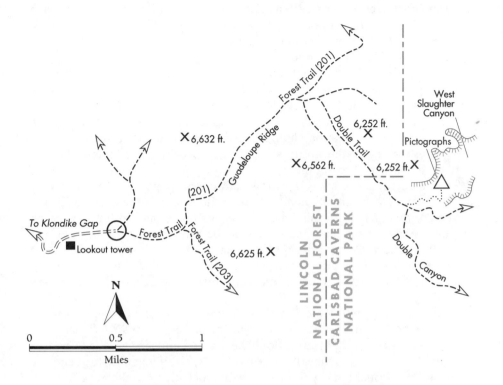

are very small. Many shapes and patterns in the artwork are also similar to pictures in Upper Grotto. Most of the pictographs in Lower Grotto are of a particular style called Chihuahuan polychrome abstract, which is found in many parts of northern Chihuahua and southern New Mexico. An exact date for the Lower Grotto artwork has not been determined, but the Chihuahuan polychrome abstract style in general is thought to predate the Mogollon occupation of the region. This would mean the majority of pictographs in Lower Grotto were made by Archaic hunter-gatherers and may be several thousand years old. Lower Painted Grotto was probably used for ceremonial purposes and shows no signs of habitation.

Given the similarities and relatively short distance between the two rock art sites, it seems reasonable to propose that most of the images in Upper Painted Grotto were also decorated by ancestors of the Mogollon. Like Lower Grotto, Upper Grotto was probably used for ceremonial purposes.

While the majority of rock art in the grottos appears to be Archaic, some pictures may have been drawn at a much later date. At least one researcher has proposed that some of the rock art in West Slaughter Canyon was made by the Apache, who arrived after the Mogollon.

Mule deer thrive throughout the Guadeloupe Mountains, and you are likely to see many of them during your hike. I also found a huge elk antler at the bottom of West Slaughter Canyon.

How to get there: Anyone with a map can figure out several ways to reach Upper Painted Grotto. However, any way you pick will require a long, hard hike. The following route was chosen because most of it follows established trails and it's all on public land.

The hiking distance is about 6.5 miles (one way). The first 3.5 miles follow a jeep trail and are relatively easy. The next 2 miles or so follow a much fainter hiking trail that in places is overgrown with heavy brush. The last mile follows no trail at all. The elevation change is about 1,100 feet. However, this is the *net* elevation change and does not consider numerous large dips that exist along the initial stretch of jeep trail. You also must drive nearly 9 miles on dirt roads, many of which are poor, to reach the "trailhead."

This is one of those hikes that looks simple on paper but becomes very confusing once you actually head into the wilderness. None of the trails are marked with signs, and trails have numerous forks that do not appear on any map I have ever seen. Some parts of the trail are very faint and often difficult to follow. Do not attempt this hike unless you know how to read a topographic map well enough that you can figure out which ridge you are on or canyon you are in at any given point during the trip. GPS will be very helpful.

There is no water in West Slaughter Canyon, so pack enough to last the entire day. Long pants are recommended for protection against brush.

This hike begins in Lincoln National Forest and ends in Carlsbad Caverns National Park. You can make the trip in one day, but if you plan to spend the night in the national park, you must obtain a permit from the Park Service. To get a permit, stop by the visitor center, which is located just off New Mexico 62, about 20 miles southwest of the city of Carlsbad. The center is open daily from 8:00 A.M. to 5:00 P.M., except during the summer when it stays open until 7:00 P.M. You can also call (505) 785-2232 and ask Park Service staff to mail you a permit.

Begin your trip by finding the community of Queen, which is west of Carlsbad Caverns National Park on NM 137. From Queen, drive southwest on NM 137 just a few miles to Guadeloupe Ridge Forest Road (FR 540). It's not paved, but it's well graded. Follow FR 540 a little more than 4 miles to Klondike Gap, which is marked with a sign. Turn left (east) onto Klondike Gap Road (FR 412-A). Parts of this road require good ground clearance. After driving a little more than 2 miles on FR 412-A, you will come to an intersection. Take a hard right turn (if you come to a fork in the road, and the road to the right is marked with a brown post bearing the numbers 9566, you have overshot the turnoff by about 0.5 mile). After turning right, the road becomes much rougher as it makes a steep climb to the top of Guadeloupe Ridge. Four-wheel drive is not needed in good weather, but high clearance is imperative all along this section of road. Continue up the mountain for roughly 2.5 miles to the Dark Canyon lookout tower, which is a fire tower.

The larger designs are red in this rock art at Upper Painted Grotto.

At the lookout tower is a jeep trail (Forest Trail 201) that continues east, then northeast, along the top of Guadeloupe Ridge. After about 0.5 mile, the jeep trail becomes so bad that it should be considered a hiking trail, so find a parking space and put your boots on or get out your sleeping bag and spend the night near your vehicle so you can begin the long hike early the following morning. There are many good places to camp along the first 0.5 mile of jeep trail, and since you are not in Carlsbad Caverns National Park yet, you don't need a permit. You cannot sleep inside the lookout tower.

The first 3 miles or so of the hike follow Forest Trail 201 northeast along the top of Guadeloupe Ridge. The road forks many times along this leg of the hike. Always stay on the widest, best-maintained road and you'll do fine. However, two major forks are not so clear. One is at the very beginning of the hike (0.5 mile east of the lookout tower). At this fork you must turn right. You will encounter the second confusing fork after hiking about 1 mile. This time veer left onto the road marked with a post bearing the number 201. The fork to the right that you are not supposed to take is Forest Trail 203.

After hiking about 3 miles from your vehicle, you will reach the beginning of the Double Trail. This will probably be the most confusing point on your entire trip. USGS topo maps would have you believe you can simply turn right off the jeep trail and head southeast down the Double Trail. In reality, you'll encounter a five-way intersection. There is a faint hiking trail that heads more or less south, paralleling the Double Trail on the west side. There is also a well-established jeep trail that parallels the Double Trail on the east side. Both of these uncharted paths are easier to find than the Double Trail. Both paths also fade away after a mile or so, but if you take either one you will end up backtracking and wasting a lot of time.

After hiking down the Double Trail a little over 2 miles, you will be very close to the bottom of West Slaughter Canyon, which will be on the left (east) side of the trail. The closer you get to West Slaughter Canyon, the more the hiking trail becomes overgrown with brush. In fact, as you get very close to the canyon, the Double Trail all but disappears. It doesn't really matter though, because you are going to have to leave the trail at some point anyway in order to reach the very bottom of West Slaughter Canyon.

So, at some point, leave the Double Trail and drop down to the bottom of West Slaughter Canyon. Once at the bottom, hike downstream (this is a figure of speech, as there is no water in the canyon). There is no trail in this portion of West Slaughter Canyon, but, compared to the terrain you just conquered, the going is relatively easy and the route is obvious. Continue down West Slaughter Canyon roughly 0.75 mile. Upper Painted Grotto will be on the right, just above the canyon bottom. The grotto, by the way, should be marked on your topo map. If by chance it's not, find an older version.

Glossary

The following definitions are tailored to this book and are to be used only in the context of hiking or archaeology of the Southwest.

Boulder Metate: Metate made in a boulder. Because of its large size, its location is permanent.

Bushwhack: To trek through the wilderness without the benefit of a road, hiking trail, or any sort of humanmade path. Bushwhacking, as it relates to hikes in this book, does not necessarily involve beating or cutting through heavy brush.

Cairn: Humanmade pile of rocks used as a trail marker. Cairns can contain anywhere from two small stones to a pile of large rocks several feet high.

Ceramics: Pottery.

Cliff Dwelling: Stone ruin built into the side of a cliff.

Granary: A small cliff dwelling used to store food.

Lithics: Tools made of stone, including arrowheads, metates, manos, and a wide range of chippers, scrapers, and hammers.

Loophole: Small "window" or peephole in the wall of a ruin.

Mano: A handheld stone, usually rectangular with rounded corners, used to grind food in a metate. The grinding motion is forward and backward.

Metate: A stone trough used to grind food, usually corn. The food is placed in a wide groove in the stone and crushed by the forward-and-backward motion of a handheld stone mano.

Mortar Hole: Similar to a metate, but the cavity in which food is placed is round instead of a straight groove. The food is ground in a circular motion with a handheld stone called a pestle. Mortar holes were also used to grind paint pigments, medicines, and pottery ingredients.

Pestle: A handheld stone used to grind food or other materials in a mortar hole. The grinding motion is circular.

Petroglyph: A prehistoric picture pecked or scratched onto a rock surface.

Pictograph: A prehistoric picture painted onto a rock surface.

Pipette: A common Hohokam petroglyph image composed of a series of squares or rectangles stacked one on top of the other, with each square or rectangle containing two smaller images, usually circles.

Potsherd (also sherd, shard, or potshard): A piece of a broken ceramic pot.

Prehistoric: Before the arrival of European-Americans. In the Southwest, this means anytime before the Spaniards showed up in A.D. 1539.

Pueblo: Stone building located on flat, open ground or on top of a hill (as opposed to being built into the side of a cliff).

Ware: A variety or family of pottery (such as plainware or black-on-white ware).

Further Reading

The following publications are referenced in this book informally by author, principal investigator, or research project.

Cosgrove, C. B. 1947. *Caves of the Upper Gila and Hueco Areas in New Mexico and Texas*. In: Papers of the Peabody Museum of American Archaeology and Ethnology, Harvard University. Vol. 24, No. 2. Published by the Peabody Museum. Includes information on ruins in the Middle Fork of the Gila River and Saddle Mountain, New Mexico.

Day, Kent C., et. al. 1963. *Moqui Canyon and Castle Wash Survey*. In: Anthropological Papers, No. 63 (Glen Canyon Series No. 18). Salt Lake City: University of Utah Press.

Gebhard, David. 1962. *Prehistoric Rock Drawings at Painted Grotto, New Mexico*. El Palacio. Vol. 69, No. 4. Santa Fe: Museum of New Mexico. Includes a very detailed description of Lower Painted Grotto.

Greenleaf, J. Cameron. 1975. *The Fortified Hill Site Near Gila Bend, Arizona*. The Kiva 40(4):213-282.

Gumerman, George J., John A. Hanson, and Carol S. Weed. 1975. *Adaptive Strategies in a Biological and Cultural Transition Zone: The Central Arizona Ecotone Project: An Interim Report*. Carbondale, Ill.: Department of Anthropology, Southern Illinois University. Contains information on ruins within the Central Arizona Ecotone Project, including a couple of sites on Perry Mesa.

Gumerman, George J., and Patricia M. Speorl. 1980. *The Hohokam and the Northern Periphery*. In: Current Issues in Hohokam Prehistory. Edited by D. E. Doyle and F. Plogg, pp. 134–50, Anthropological Research Paper No. 23. Tempe: Arizona State University. More information on the Central Arizona Ecotone Project.

_____. 1984. *Prehistoric Cultural Development in Central Arizona: Archaeology of the Upper New River Region*. Occasional Paper No. 5. Carbondale: Carbondale Center for Archaeological Investigations, Southern Illinois University. Still more information on the Central Arizona Ecotone Project.

Gunnerson, James. 1962. *Archaeological Survey in the Hammond Canyon Area, Southeastern Utah*. In: Anthropological Papers, No. 60. Salt Lake City: University of Utah Press.

Haury, Emil W. 1934. *The Canyon Creek Ruin and the Cliff Dwellings of the Sierra Ancha*. Medallion Papers, 14. Globe, Ariz.: Gila Pueblo.

Hewett, Edgar L. 1906. *Antiquities of the Jemez Plateau, New Mexico*. Washington, D.C.: Government Printing Office. Contains information about sites in Bandelier National Monument, including Yapashi Ruin, the Stone Lions shrine, and the Painted Cave.

_____. 1909. *The Pajaritan Culture*. Archaeological Institute of America: Papers of the School of American Archaeology No.3. Santa Fe: Museum of New Mexico. Contains general information about the Pajaritan culture of Bandelier National Monument.

_____. 1938. *Pajarito Plateau and Its Ancient People*. Albuquerque: The University of New Mexico Press. Contains information about sites in Bandelier National Monument, including Yapashi Ruin, the Stone Lions shrine, and the Painted Cave.

Hewett, Edgar L., and Wayne L. Mauzy. 1953. *Landmarks of New Mexico*. Albuquerque: New Mexico Press. Contains information about sites in Bandelier National Monument, including Yapashi Pueblo, the Stone Lions shrine, and the Painted Cave.

Hohmann, John W., and Linda B. Kelley. 1988. *Erich F. Schmidt's Investigations of Salado Sites in Central Arizona*. Series 56. Flagstaff, Ariz.: The Museum of Northern Arizona Bulletin.

Holiday, William G. 1974. *Archaeological Investigations in the Cave Creek Drainage, Tonto National Forest, Arizona*. Archaeological Report No. 1. Albuquerque: Southwest Region, USDA Forest Service.

Holmlund, James P., and Henry D. Wallace. 1986. *Petroglyphs of the Picacho Mountains, South Central Arizona*. Anthropological Papers 6. Tucson: Institute for American Research.

Hough, Walter. 1907. *Antiquities of the Upper Gila and Salt River Valleys in Arizona and New Mexico*. In: Smithsonian Institution Bureau of American Ethnology, Bulletin 35. Washington, D.C.: Government Printing Office. Contains a reference to the Saddle Mountain cliff dwelling.

Johnson, Alfred E. 1963. *An Appraisal of the Archaeological Resources of Five Regional Parks in Maricopa County, Arizona*. Tucson: Arizona State Museum. Includes results of an archaeological survey conducted in Waterfall Canyon.

Judd, Neil M. 1926. *Archaeological Observations North of the Rio Colorado*. Smithsonian Institution Bureau of American Ethnology, Bulletin 82. Washington, D.C.: Government Printing Office. Includes information on the archaeology of Cottonwood Canyon near Kanab, Utah.

Manje, Juan Mateo (1693–1721). *Luz de la Tierra Incógnita: Unknown Arizona and Sonora: An English Translation of Part II*. Harry J. Karns and Associates. 1954. Tucson: Arizona Silhouettes. Includes a reference to the Gila River having a lot of water in the sixteenth century. Also includes a description of how Pima Indians used a special type of "fortified hilltop" for defense.

Mera, H. P. 1938. *Reconnaissance and Excavation in Southeastern New Mexico*. Memoirs of the American Anthropological Association, No. 51. Includes a very brief description and interpretation of Lower Painted Grotto (called Painted Cave by Mera).

Schaafsma, Polly. 1992. *Rock Art in New Mexico*. Santa Fe: Museum of New Mexico Press. Includes a reference to rock art in the Middle Fork of the Gila River, plus a very detailed description of Lower Painted Grotto in Carlsbad Caverns National Park.

Schwartz, Douglas W. 1963. *An Archaeological Survey of Nankoweap Canyon, Grand Canyon National Park*. In: American Antiquity. Vol. 28, No. 3, Society for American Archaeology.

Schwartz, Douglas W. 1963. *On the Edge of Splendor: Exploring Grand Canyon's Human Past*. Annual Bulletin of the School of American Research. Includes general information about the archaeology of the Grand Canyon, including a reference to the Nankoweap area.

Valehrach, Emil M. 1967. *A Site on the Verde*. The Arizona Archaeologist, No. 1: 25–34. This paper was written about St. Clair Mountain (Brazaletes Pueblo) but is much less involved than Valehrach's 1971 report.

Valehrach, Emil M., and Bruce S. Valehrach. 1971. *Excavations at Brazaletes Pueblo*. The Arizona Archaeologist, No. 6.

Wasley, William W., and Alfred E. Johnson. 1965. *Salvage Archaeology in Painted Rocks Reservoir, Western Arizona*. Anthropological Papers of the University of Arizona, No. 9. Includes information about petroglyphs in the Gila Bend Mountains.

Weaver, Donald E., Jr. 1985. *Hieroglyphic Canyon: A Petroglyph Record of a Changing Subsistence Pattern*. Monograph 1. El Toro, Calif.: American Rock Art Research Association. Monograph 1.

ADDITIONAL SOURCES

The following is a partial list of additional sources that were not referenced in this book.

Adair, Malcolm, Richard V. N. Ahlstrom, Robert C. Euler, and R. Thomas Euler. 1992. *Pothunting in Central Arizona: The Perry Mesa Archaeological Site Vandalism Study*. In: Cultural Resource Management, Report No. 13. USDA Forest Service, Southwest Region, and USDI Bureau of Land Management, Arizona.

Arizona State Historic Preservation Office. 1987. *Archaeology and the Law: Archaeological Resources Protection Act of 1979: Arizona Felony Conviction Is a First; Proposed Amendments May Strengthen Antivandalism Efforts*. In: Arizona Archaeological Council Newsletter. Vol. 11, No 4, p. 3. Provides an overview of the Archaeological Resources Protection Act along with information on the first person convicted as a criminal under the act.

_____. 1988. *Archaeology and the Law: Arizona Antiquities Enact One of Strongest Laws for Protecting Prehistoric and Historic Cultural Resources: Establishes Procedures and Penalties*. In: Arizona Archaeological Council Newsletter. Vol. 12, No 1, p. 3.

Bannister, Bryant, and William J. Robinson. 1971. *Tree-Ring Dates from Arizona UW: Gila Salt Rivers Area*. Tucson: Laboratory of Tree-Ring Research, University of Arizona. Gives cutting dates for wooden beams used in the construction of many cliff dwellings in the Sierra Ancha.

Christenson, Andrew L. 1991. *The Microenvironment of Cliff Dwellings in Tsegi Canyon, Arizona*. The Kiva 57(1):39–54. Gives results of research that shows cliff dwellings provide protection from moisture.

Ciolek-Torrello, Richard S., and Richard C. Lange. 1982. *Archaeology of the Sierra Ancha: A Synthesis of the Gila Pueblo Survey*. In: Introduction and Special Studies, pp. 95–126. Cholla Project Archaeology. Vol. 1. Edited by J. Jefferson Reid. Tucson: Arizona State Museum Archaeological Series, No. 161. Tucson: University of Arizona. Includes information about many cliff dwellings in the Sierra Ancha.

_____. 1990. *The Gila Pueblo Survey of Southeastern Sierra Ancha*. The Kiva 55(2):127–54. Includes information about many cliff dwellings in the Sierra Ancha.

Day, Kent C., et. al. 1966. *An Archaeological Survey of Canyonlands National Park*. In: Anthropological Papers, No. 83. Salt Lake City: University of Utah Press. Includes general information about the archaeology of Salt Creek, including a reference to artifacts obtained from the Big Ruin. Also discusses the Fremont influence on ancestral Pueblo rock art.

Dean, Jeffrey S. 1986. *Tse Yaa Kin: Houses Beneath the Rock*. Exploration: Annual Bulletin of the School of American Research. Santa Fe, New Mexico. Contains information about cliff dwellings throughout the Southwest and explains some leading theories about why the Native Americans built them.

Dean, Jeffrey S., and William J. Robinson. 1969. *Tree-Ring Dates from Utah S-W*. Tucson: Laboratory of Tree Ring Research, University of Arizona. Includes tree-ring dates for some ruins in Grand Gulch.

Domenici. 1988. *Theft of Our Nation's Archaeological Resources*. Congressional Record–Senate. June 15, 1988 (legislative day of June 13). 100th Congress, 2nd Session. Vol. 134, No. 88. This is a transcript of a speech given by the man who drafted the Archaeological Resources Protection Act in 1979. The speech briefly explains the act, addresses the problem of archaeological theft, and calls upon Congress to enact stiffer penalties for violators.

Effland, Richard W., Jr., and Barbara S. Macnider. 1991. *An Overview of the Cultural Heritage of the Tonto National Forest*. Tempe, Ariz.: Archaeological Consulting Services, Ltd. Cultural Resources Report No. 49. Includes, among many other things, an overview of the prehistory of Perry Mesa.

Ferg, Allan, et al. 1979. *A Summary of Conclusions and Recommendations of the Tumamoc Hill Survey*. The Kiva 45(1–2):187–95. An overview of several research projects conducted on Tumamoc Hill in the Tucson Mountains, including David Wilcox's work with a certain type of "fortified hilltop."

Griffin, Dennis P. 1984. *Archaeological Inventory in the Salt Creek Archaeological District, Canyonlands National Park*. Lincoln, Neb.: Midwest Archaeological Center, National Park Service, United States Department of the Interior. Includes a reference to the Salt Creek area containing larger ruins than surrounding areas in Canyonlands National Park because of the availability of water.

Haas, Jonathan, and David R. Wilcox. 1994. *Scream of the Butterfly*. In: Themes in Southwest Prehistory. Edited by George J. Gumerman. Santa Fe: School of American Research Press. Addresses the issue of warfare in the prehistoric Southwest. Includes discussions of many types of prehistoric ruins thought to have been built for defense.

Hibben, Frank C. 1948. *The Gallina Architectural Forms*. In: American Antiquity. Vol. 14, No. 1. Society for American Archaeology. Includes a description of the Nogales Cliff House in Spring (Nogales) Canyon in the Santa Fe National Forest.

_____. 1948. *The Gallina Phase*. In: American Antiquity. Society for American Archaeology. Vol. 14, No. 3. Includes general information about prehistoric Pueblo Indians in the vicinity of the Nogales Cliff House in Spring (Nogales) Canyon in the Santa Fe National Forest.

Hirschmann, Fred, and Scott Thybony. *Rock Art of the American Southwest*. Portland, Ore.: Graphic Arts Center Publishing Company. Includes a sequence of pictures showing how a spiral petroglyph functions as a solstice marker.

Hohmann, John W. 1985. *Archaeological Evidence for Raiding and Warfare in Central Arizona: A Salado Example*. Paper presented to the 29th Annual Meeting of the Arizona-Nevada Academy of Science, Las Vegas, Nevada. Discusses bundles of human limbs found in the Tonto basin that are thought to be trophies of Salado warfare.

Hoskinson, Tom. 1990. *Lightning Strikes Incorporated into Southwestern Gila River Rock Art Designs*. In: Rock Art Papers, edited by Ken Hedges. Vol. 7, pp. 103–109. San Diego Museum Papers 26. Includes evidence that a spiral petroglyph near Gila Bend marks a place to observe the solstice. Also provides evidence that a petroglyph near Gila Bend shaped like the sun (a "sunflower") marks a place to observe the solstice.

Hutt, Sherry, Martin E. McAllister, and Elwood W. Jones. 1992. *Archaeological Resource Protection*. Baltimore, Md.: Port City Press. Includes the actual Archaeological Resources Protection Act of 1979 as it was written by lawmakers.

Jacka, Jerry D. 1978. *Prehistoric Sites of Perry Mesa*. In: MNA Research Paper No. 11, pp. 271–82. Flagstaff, Ariz.: Museum of Northern Arizona.

Martynec, Richard. 1989. *Hohokam, Patayan, or ?: Rock Art at Two Sites Near Gila Bend, Arizona*. In: Ken Hedges, ed., Rock Art Papers. Vol. 6, pp. 17–116. San Diego Museum Papers No. 24. Includes information about petroglyphs at the Gila Bend ruin (Fortified Hill).

Patterson, Alex. 1992. *A Field Guide to Rock Art Symbols of the Greater Southwest*. Boulder, Colo.: Johnson Printing Company. Provides interpretations of many petroglyph designs, including spirals, stars (outlined crosses), and swastikas.

Robinson, William J., and Richard L. Warren. 1971. *Tree-Ring Dates from New Mexico C-D*. Tucson: Laboratory of Tree Ring Research, University of Arizona. Includes tree-ring dates for Nogales Cliff House in Spring (Nogales) Canyon in the Santa Fe National Forest.

Rohn, Arthur H., et. al. 1989. *Rock Art of Bandelier National Monument*. Albuquerque: University New Mexico Press. Contains information about sites in Bandelier National Monument, including the Painted Cave and Stone Lions shrine.

Stoney, Stephen A. 1988. *Sun, Sandstone, and Shadow: Rock Art in Southern Nevada Takes on New Meaning*. In: Ken Hedges, ed., Rock Art Papers. Vol. 8, pp. 103–110. San Diego Museum Papers 27. Provides evidence that a star-shaped (outlined cross) petroglyph in Nevada functions as a solstice marker.

Stuart, David E. 1989. *The Magic of Bandelier*. Santa Fe: Ancient City Press. Contains information about sites in Bandelier National Monument, including Yapashi ruin and the Stone Lions shrine.

Taylor, Walter W. 1958. *Two Archaeological Studies in Northern Arizona*. Flagstaff, Ariz.: Northern Arizona Society of Science and Art. Includes a description of the Nankoweap cliff dwelling in the Grand Canyon.

White, J. Courtney. 1992. *In the Land of the Delight Makers: An Archaeological Survey in the American West.* Salt Lake City: University of Utah Press. Contains a small amount of information about Yapashi Ruin and the Stone Lions shrine in Bandelier National Monument.

Wilcox, David R. 1979. *Warfare Implications of Dry-Laid Masonry Walls on Tumamoc Hill.* The Kiva 45:15–38. Presents a theory that a certain type of fortified hilltop in the Tucson Mountains was used for defense and proposes that a "tribute system" may have existed between the Hohokam in the core area and the Hohokam on the periphery.

Wood, J. Scott. 1994. *Field Trip to Perry Mesa.* Phoenix: Tonto National Forest. A great summary of the archaeology of Perry Mesa, written in plain English. Includes drawings of the ruins that show how all the rooms are laid out.

Index

About the Author

Dave Wilson grew up in Tucson and earned a degree in journalism with a minor in wildlife science from the University of Arizona. After graduating he moved to Phoenix and worked for several years as a writer for a public relations agency that promotes manufacturers in the outdoor-recreation industry. Dave also spent a couple of years writing corporate newsletters for a diverse array of companies across the nation and currently writes for a bimonthly newspaper in downtown Mesa, Arizona.

While in Tucson, Dave spent much time hiking in the mountains around the city and photographing wildlife. His pictures of deer, javelina, bighorn sheep, and other desert creatures have appeared on his own line of greeting cards. After moving to the state capital, Dave discovered that Phoenix was the center of the great prehistoric culture of the Hohokam. Every mountain range around the "Valley of the Sun" was filled with ruins and petroglyphs, many of which were in remote areas and made great hiking destinations. Dave simply changed lenses and began hunting for archaeological sites to photograph instead of animals.

Dave eventually combined his interests in Native American ruins and the outdoors with his passion for writing and photography by creating *Hiking Ruins Seldom Seen.* This is a guide for hiking and finding off-the-beaten-path ruins and rock art sites from southern Utah, to the Grand Canyon, through central and southern Arizona, and into New Mexico. It is a book for outdoor enthusiasts, amateur archaeologists, and anyone with an adventurous spirit and desire to see some of the wilder parts of the American Southwest.

Notes

Notes

Notes

Notes

FALCONGUIDES® Leading the Way

Come to America's wilderness areas and enjoy some of the most pristine hiking conditions you'll ever experience. With FalconGuides you'll be able to plan your trip, including learning how to get there, getting a permit, if necessary, and picking your campsites. Types of trails, difficulty ratings, distances, maps, elevation charts, and backcountry regulations are covered in detail. You'll also learn "zero impact" principles, safety tips, and other essential information specific to the wilderness area you visit. The following titles are currently available, and this list grows every year. For a free catalog with a complete list of titles, call The Globe Pequot Press toll-free at 1–800–243–0495.

Hiking the Beartooths
Hiking the Bob Marshall Country
Hiking Colorado's Weminuche Wilderness
Hiking Oregon's Central Cascades
Hiking Oregon's Eagle Cap Wilderness
Hiking Oregon's Mount Hood & Badger Creek Wilderness
Hiking Wyoming's Cloud Peak Wilderness
Hiking Wyoming's Wind River Range
Wild Montana
Wild Utah

Wilderness area FalconGuides® are published in cooperation with *The Wilderness Society*

To order any of these books, check with your local bookseller, or call The Globe Pequot Press at **1–800–243–0495.**
Visit us on the world wide web at:
www.falcon.com

FALCONGUIDES ® Leading the Way™

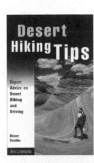

DESERT HIKING TIPS
By Bruce Grubbs
This pocket-sized book explains how to enjoy hiking and exploring the American desert.

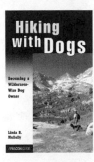

HIKING WITH DOGS
by Linda Mullally
This comprehensive hiking guide highlights the benefits of hiking with your dog while helping readers choose, train, condition and care for their canine hiking companions.

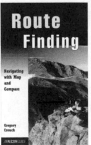

ROUTE FINDING
by Gregory Crouch
Explains step-by-step the map reading, land navigation, and route finding techniques crucial to success and safety in the outdoors.

Also Available:
Avalanche Aware, Backpacking Tips, Bear Aware,
Zero Impact, Mountain Lion Alert, Reading Weather, Using GPS, Wild
Country Companion, Wilderness First Aid, Wilderness Survival

To order these titles, check with your local bookseller or
call The Globe Pequot Press at **1-800-243-0495.**
www.falcon.com

FALCONGUIDES® Leading the Way™

HIKING GUIDES

Best Hikes Along the Continental Divide
Hiking Alaska
Hiking Arizona
Hiking Arizona's Cactus Country
Hiking the Beartooths
Hiking Big Bend National Park
Hiking the Bob Marshall Country
Hiking California
Hiking California's Desert Parks
Hiking Carlsbad Caverns
  and Guadalupe Mtns. National Parks
Hiking Colorado
Hiking Colorado, Vol. II
Hiking Colorado's Summits
Hiking Colorado's Weminuche Wilderness
Hiking the Columbia River Gorge
Hiking Florida
Hiking Georgia
Hiking Glacier & Waterton Lakes National Parks
Hiking Grand Canyon National Park
Hiking Grand Staircase-Escalante/Glen Canyon
Hiking Grand Teton National Park
Hiking Great Basin National Park
Hiking Hot Springs in the Pacific Northwest
Hiking Idaho
Hiking Maine
Hiking Michigan
Hiking Minnesota
Hiking Montana
Hiking Mount Rainier National Park
Hiking Mount St. Helens
Hiking Nevada
Hiking New Hampshire

Hiking New Mexico
Hiking New York
Hiking the North Cascades
Hiking Northern Arizona
Hiking Olympic National Park
Hiking Oregon
Hiking Oregon's Eagle Cap Wilderness
Hiking Oregon's Mount Hood/Badger Creek
Hiking Oregon's Three Sisters Country
Hiking Pennsylvania
Hiking Ruins Seldom Seen
Hiking Shenandoah
Hiking the Sierra Nevada
Hiking South Carolina
Hiking South Dakota's Black Hills Country
Hiking Southern New England
Hiking Tennessee
Hiking Texas
Hiking Utah
Hiking Utah's Summits
Hiking Vermont
Hiking Virginia
Hiking Washington
Hiking Wisconsin
Hiking Wyoming
Hiking Wyoming's Cloud Peak Wilderness
Hiking Wyoming's Wind River Range
Hiking Yellowstone National Park
Hiking Zion & Bryce Canyon National Parks
Wild Montana
Wild Country Companion
Wild Utah
Wild Virginia

■ *To order any of these books, check with your local bookseller,*
or call The Globe Pequot Press at **1-800-243-0495.**
Visit us on the world wide web at:
www.falcon.com

FALCON®